CONSUMER GUIDE®

BEST RATED
REAL ESTATE
INVESTMENTS

Printed in Canada

Authors: C. Randall Pivar and William H. Pivar
Cover Design: Michael Johnson

C. Randall Pivar is a successful real estate investor who
started his real estate investment program while a college
student. In addition to managing his own properties, he has
counseled many successful investors.

Dr. William H. Pivar is a professor of business education at
College of the Desert, a California State College. He is the
author of ten real estate books, and he serves as a consultant
for a number of major real estate firms.

TABLE OF
CONTENTS

INTRODUCTION

Real estate investments have created more millionaires than any other investment or business. Generation after generation has learned that real estate can be the key to financial security and peace of mind.

Besides providing such tangible benefits as income and tax advantages, real estate provides an intangible sense of worth and well-being. To be a land or property owner is to participate in a tradition that is nearly as old as mankind.

Real estate investments are not just for those who are already rich. Real estate investment is a game anyone can play. You can embark on a program of real estate investment regardless of your age, credit history, or resources.

What you need to do first is arm yourself with essential information—information that you will find within these pages. Like any area of investment, real estate has its own language. Beginning investors are sometimes discouraged by the words and terms they may be encountering for the first time. But by learning the most important and most common elements of that language,

INTRODUCTION

you'll be comfortable and prepared as you enter the world of real estate investment.

Throughout this publication, you'll find practical tips that will help you make the best and most informed real estate investment decisions. You'll learn many of the tax ramifications of real estate, how to turn your home into a successful investment, and the benefits—and pitfalls—of becoming a landlord.

Perhaps you are more interested in commercial or industrial property, or in purchasing older homes for rehab and conversion. Other options are offered by Real Estate Investment Trusts (REITs) and Real Estate Limited Partnerships (RELPs). The possibilities are almost endless.

A vital consideration, though, is that not all real estate investments are suited for all real estate investors. This publication provides a great deal more information than just the basics of how to invest. It is a working tool to use in locating and securing the best real estate investments possible—investments that are tailored to your own personal needs and goals. No other investor has precisely the same needs and desires as you. Personal and financial situations differ. Additionally, your investment needs will change throughout your life—one's financial status and even investment philosophy are far from static.

INTRODUCTION

One of the many positive things about real estate is that, unlike some other investments, it is flexible and capable of change. You can alter land or other real property so that it will conform with your present and future needs. The choice is yours; through real estate investments you can secure your future today, and avoid having to react to the future tomorrow.

THE BEST INVESTMENT REAL ESTATE—

The saddest thing to hear is "I should have purchased real estate back in...." Many people lament what they should have done but fail to consider what they should be *doing*.

There are so many real estate properties on the market owned by so many people with different needs and motivations that excellent investment opportunities are always available for those willing to look for them. These opportunities exist in every economic climate.

The benefits of real estate include low risk, income, appreciation, leverage opportunities, as well as tax advantages. You must learn to think of real estate investments in terms of your own personal needs. The best real estate investment for someone else might not be a proper investment for you.

RISK

While every investment carries with it some degree of risk, properly selected investments expose the investor to minimum risks. If we consider foreclosure rates we can see that in most areas of the nation less than 3 percent of mortgages given

THE BEST INVESTMENT

are foreclosed. This means that over 97 percent of the property owners were able to honor their commitments. The advice in this book can be expected to reduce your investment risk significantly below the average risk.

While real estate values have fallen during economic recessions, the drop in value has been significantly less than losses suffered by other investment alternatives. In many economic downturns real estate values have actually increased, with the greatest increases experienced by the better investments. A reason for this seeming inconsistency is that demand actually increased because of investors selling other securities and seeking the safety and relative stability of real estate.

Because real estate is so widely owned, the real estate market operates on pure economics of supply and demand. The huge numbers of owners and potential buyers protect the real estate market from the manipulations of a few.

Real estate loans are *amortized*. This means that loans are fully liquidated by equal monthly payments. Because the amount of the loan decreases with each payment, the risk also decreases. Even without appreciation there is a steady increase in owner's equity.

While no investor likes to think negatively, in many states there is no personal liability of the investor for losses should a property be fore-closed. In others, a deficiency judgment (a court judgment that the borrower is liable for the deficiency amount) is difficult or unlikely to be granted. A local attorney can tell you about your state laws.

INCOME

You will find many real estate investments pro-viding income equal to or better than available alternative investments. In addition, increased value can lead to future increases in income that can far exceed fixed income investments.

APPRECIATION

Our supply of land is relatively inelastic. This means we are dealing with a fixed supply. When demand increases without a corresponding in-crease in supply, prices rise. We call this a *demand pull inflation*. In growing communities, we see increasing demand resulting in higher values. The values that will increase the most will be for those properties and in those areas in which de-mand will show the greatest increase.

Besides demand pull inflation we also have *cost push inflation*. Increasing costs of labor and ma-terial will cause the price of new construction to rise. When new construction costs increase, existing property will show a corresponding increase in value.

During an inflationary period the value of money decreases in terms of purchasing power. The true value of money in fixed-income accounts actually decreases. Because of the interrelated actions of demand pull and cost push inflation on real estate, the value of real estate has historically increased significantly more than the inflation factor. This is why real estate is considered to be the best hedge against inflation.

PYRAMIDING

Appreciation allows real estate investors to pyramid their holdings as equity increases due to inflation, improvements, management, and debt reduction. Properties can be sold and the proceeds used to buy even larger properties. A great many owners of multi-million dollar properties pyramided their way to riches after starting with a single-family home or duplex.

Another way to pyramid is to use the equity developed to buy other properties. By borrowing on the equity it is possible to milk cash from a property without selling it.

LEVERAGE

It is possible to use other people's money to your advantage when investing in real estate. Most real estate investments are *leveraged,* which simply means that loans are used to purchase real property. If a person pays 10 percent down and the property increases 10 percent in value, because of the leverage the investor has a 100 percent increase in equity. If the same person had paid all cash, a 10 percent increase in value would simply provide a 10 percent increase in the investor's equity.

Even without any appreciation, leverage offers exceptional opportunities. If an investor goes one million dollars into debt to purchase a property and the income is sufficient to pay the debt service, the investor's net worth would have increased by one million dollars when the loan is paid off.

TAX BENEFITS

Any real estate investment should make economic sense. An investor should consider degrees of risk, present income, and anticipated future income, as well as appreciation in value. Tax benefits should be considered a bonus. If an investment does not make economic sense without tax benefits you should consider looking further for an investment opportunity.

Tax benefits of real estate as an investment include depreciation that shelters income from taxation, and capital gains, which reduce the tax liability when a gain is realized.

THE BEST INVESTMENT

DEPRECIATION

While land cannot be depreciated, improvements to land which are used for income or investment purposes *can* be depreciated. Depreciation is an accounting expense that reduces income. It is not a cash expense.

Assume a property has an annual income of $50,000 and total cash expenses of $45,000. This property would leave the owner with a spendable net of $5,000. If the property also had $10,000 in depreciation, the property would have $55,000 in expenses and a loss of $10,000. This paper loss would mean that not only would the $5,000 spendable cash not be taxed, but that another $5,000 of the taxpayer's income would also be sheltered from taxation.

For tax purposes, real property can currently be depreciated over 19 years. The most common method of depreciation is the straight line method. Under this method the property would be depreciated 1/19th of its value, or approximately 5.25 percent per year. If the cost attributed to the improvements were $100,000, the annual depreciation would be $5,250 per year for 19 years.

It is possible to get greater depreciation in the early years by using an accelerated depreciation method known as the 175 percent declining balance method. Before you use the declining balance method you should consult an accountant;

if you sell the property prior to fully depreciating it, you will be subject to *recapture* penalties, with which the IRS will tax (recapture) depreciation that was taken as if it were regular income.

As an astute investor you will want to get the greatest depreciation possible. Because land cannot be depreciated, you would want to allocate the greatest possible amount of your purchase price to the improvements and the least possible amount to the land. In most areas, tax assessors tend to show a relatively small percentage of the total assessed value for the land. If this is the case, use the assessor's ratio of land value to total assessed value and apply this ratio to your purchase price. As an example, assume a tax assessor assessed the land at $10,000 and the improvements at $90,000, making the total assessed valuation $100,000.

Land value	**$ 10,000**
Total value	**$100,000**

The assessed land value is 10 percent of total assessed valuation. If you paid $280,000 for this property you could use this same ratio by assigning 10 percent, ($28,000) to the land and 90 percent ($252,000) to the improvements. Even though the value assigned to the land might be unrealistically low, the IRS will generally accept the apportionment in value made by a government agency.

THE BEST INVESTMENT

If you feel the percentage of value attributable to the land based on the tax appraisal is high, you can use a fee appraiser and base your improvement value on the appraisal received.

CAPITAL GAINS

While wages and business profits are fully taxable, long-term capital gains are given preferential tax treatment. Capital gains are profits from the sale of capital assets that have been held more than six months for the purpose of business or investment. The gain is computed by the difference between the book value and the sale price. Book value is your cost plus improvements, less the depreciation you've taken.

Currently, 60 percent of a long-term capital gain is exempt from income taxation. The other 40 percent of the gain is added to your regular income. Since the maximum individual tax rate is 50 percent, the most any taxpayer would ever have to pay would be 20 percent of the gain (50 percent of 40 percent). For most taxpayers this amount would be considerably less.

Assume an investor purchased a property for $100,000 and depreciated it down to $50,000. A later sale at $100,000 would mean a gain of $50,000. This actually could have been an excellent investment. Regular income of $50,000 was not taxed when it was earned because it was offset by depreciation. After having the use of the nontaxed income, the investor now must pay a tax, but only 40 percent of the gain is now taxed, with 60 percent exempt.

Our income tax is progressive, which means that the lower portions of our income are taxed at a lower rate; as our income increases, the highest portion is taxed at a higher rate. Therefore, taking a large capital gain in one year would boost income into higher tax brackets. If, however, the taxpayer were to get only a portion of the gain in the year of the sale, only that portion received would be taxed in that year. The seller, by financing the buyer, can thus keep total tax liability at a minimum by spreading out the capital gains over a number of years. Sellers contemplating retirement could realize significant tax savings by taking the greatest portion of their gain when they might have significantly lower income.

TAX REFORM

There have been a number of tax reform proposals which could reduce the tax benefits of real estate. A likely tax change is a longer period for depreciation.

Other proposals include limitation on interest deductions, doing away with capital gains as we now know it, and lowering tax brackets that reduce the advantage of real estate over other investments. These proposals are unlikely to be enacted because at least 80 percent of our Congress would be adversely affected by them.

PSYCHIC INCOME

Ownership of land and buildings provides owners with an intangible benefit—a psychic income. There is a sense of pride, permanence, and security in owning real property; passbooks and paper securities fail to provide these benefits. This psychic income, while not bankable, can go a long way to increase the quality of and satisfaction with your life.

NEGATIVE INCOME

No one likes a negative cash flow, which arises when cash expenses exceed cash receipts. While negative cash flows should generally be avoided, strong economic factors sometimes turn a negative cash flow property into a wise investment.

Properties where rents can be increased, or where below-market leases will expire offer opportunities that can turn a negative cash flow investment into a strong net spendable income.

If a present use is not consistent with the best use of the property, there will likely be a negative cash flow. Investors might consider such a situation as temporary, since redevelopment of the property to a use consistent with its land value could eliminate the negative cash flow.

WHY PEOPLE DON'T INVEST IN REAL ESTATE

Many would-be real estate investors are turned off after talking to friends. If your friends are not investing in real estate themselves, they most certainly will not advise you to get into real estate investments. To do so would force them to admit that they are not wise in financial management.

Never ask your banker for advice about real estate investments. This is especially true if you have a low-interest account in his or her bank. Your banker makes a profit on your money; the last thing a banker wants is to see money leaving the bank. Your banker is likely to suggest that you invest in a nice long-term certificate of deposit. There *are* people whose advice you *should* seek; these include accountants and attorneys.

ACCOUNTANTS

Accountants understand the benefits of capital gains, depreciation, and installment sales. Generally, accountants can give you good advice as to what you should look for in investments. Ac-

THE BEST INVESTMENT

countants make good friends, too, since they often like to talk shop, even on social occasions. There is a great deal that you can learn from them which will help you.

ATTORNEYS

Before you enter into real estate agreements, an attorney should be consulted as to the legal significance. While attorneys' expertise is in the law, many attorneys do not limit their advice to legal rights and obligations. While you should certainly listen to your attorney, keep in mind that the decision as to what property you should buy, how much you should pay, and how you should pay it are decisions which should not be delegated to others.

RECORD KEEPING

Salaried people may be put off on real estate investing because of the record keeping involved. Actually, record keeping can be simplified by opening a separate checking account for your investment property. This eliminates the need for extensive bookwork, and makes year-end tax accounting quite simple. Investors with a number of properties often use separate checking accounts for each property.

THE BEST INVESTMENT

LEARNING

The hard-knocks school of real estate education allows you to learn by your mistakes. While this method of education may be effective it can also be costly. A far better way is to take your time and carefully study the market and properties.

Vocational schools, community colleges, and even four-year colleges offer real estate courses that can help make you a better investor. Some of the basic courses valuable to investors include Real Estate Principles, Real Estate Appraisal, and Real Estate Finance. By checking various schools, you will likely find offerings in Real Estate Investment, Syndication, Subdivisions, Urban Economics, and other specialized areas. Education will serve to reduce your risk and maximize the profits of your investment.

YOUR HOME—
THE BEST
FIRST INVESTMENT

The first goal of all real estate investors should be owning their own home. A home of your own provides more than shelter. It provides a quality of life and sense of security not possible in renting. It is also a sound investment. The high loan-to-value-ratio loans available for owner-occupied housing, as well as the availability of creative financing, make home ownership possible for most working Americans.

LOCATION

It is often stated that the three most important elements of value for real property are location, location, and location. Your home should be in the most desirable location that you can afford. With an inflation rate of just 3 percent, it won't be long before your payments will seem very modest.

The rate of appreciation in value as well as the time it takes to resell are both related directly to location. The most desirable locations can expect the greatest appreciation in value, as well as the shortest time on the resale market.

YOUR HOME AS AN INVESTMENT

A property in an area of more expensive properties will increase in value because of the properties around it. This is known as the principle of *progression*. A modest home in a neighborhood of more expensive homes would therefore have a value greater than it would have in a neighborhood of homes similar to it. Conversely, a quality home in an area of less-expensive homes would have its value decreased because of the properties around it. This is the principle of *regression*. You probably can identify homes which would be worth a great deal more if they were in areas having homes of similar quality.

The principle of regression also applies to improving your home. Costly overimprovements, so that a home becomes the finest in the area, might give an owner a sense of pride; but when it comes to resale the owner might not be able to recoup the value of the improvements. Before making extensive improvements, view them on an economic basis. An owner would often be better off selling, and buying a finer house in a neighborhood of more expensive homes than making major improvements to an existing home.

A LOCAL MARKET

The real estate market for housing is relatively localized. Similar housing in similar areas within

30 or 40 miles of each other might sell at dissimilar prices. Because of the local nature of the real estate market, many people choose to commute great distances to work in order to afford the quality of housing that they desire.

HOME STYLES

Even though you might be buying a home primarily to improve your quality of life, you should consider saleability. Traditional home styles generally show the greatest appreciation in value and are most desired by buyers. Colonial, Tudor, or Elizabethan styles are in great demand. In the Southwest, Spanish styles are desired.

While people love to look at extremes in architecture and floor plans, they tend to buy much more conservatively. Unique housing generally takes longer to sell and must often be sold at less than reproduction cost.

Similarly, a home which lacks a feature desired by most buyers in an area will present resale difficulties. If most of the buyers in an area expect a private bath off of the master bedroom, a home which does not have this feature might be difficult to sell without a significant price concession.

NEW HOMES

There are several advantages to buying new homes, including lower maintenance costs and excellent financing, often secured by the developer. When developments are completed, new homes generally show excellent appreciation. Particular builders within your area will have likely developed a positive reputation. Homes built by these builders will be more desirable when you decide to sell.

OLDER HOMES

The distinctive nature and quality construction of older homes is being rediscovered. Besides being spacious, older homes can often be purchased at prices significantly less than new, smaller tract homes.

Neighborhoods take on an even greater importance when considering an older home. You want one which is either in a stable neighborhood or one that is undergoing a positive change.

The greatest appreciation possibilities are in areas that are showing improvement. These are usually areas formerly occupied by upper-middle class residents but which over the years became areas of low-cost housing. Examples of positive change would be recent sales to people whose income and/or education level is significantly higher than those of the majority of other residents. A block which has seen the restoration of four or five older homes would be an area to consider. At the present time, Victorian styles are in great demand and are likely to show exceptional appreciation.

YOUR HOME AS AN INVESTMENT

It would be wise to pay a builder to inspect an older home prior to purchase. You want to know what you are getting into before you are obligated to buy. Wiring may be inadequate and plumbing may need extensive repair. Insulation work may also be needed. If there is an old coal furnace with an oil or gas conversion, it is likely to be inefficient—replacement should be considered.

MOBILE HOMES

Mobile homes offer inexpensive housing but are a much lower-quality investment than conventional housing. While mobile homes in desirable parks have increased in value, the increase has generally been far less than the appreciation in value of conventional housing.

In many cases, mobile homes lose value. Older single-wide units can be difficult to sell even at low prices. In some cases park owners, wishing to update their parks, require these older units to be removed when sold.

The owner of a mobile home is unable to lock in housing costs. Park rentals have experienced dramatic increases. Because larger double- and triple-wide units can be moved only at great expense, owners are forced to pay the increase.

On the plus side, favorable mobile home financing is often available (sometimes including the furnishings). Mobile homes do make excellent weekend or vacation homes, as well as rental units.

CONDOMINIUMS

Condominium ownership is not for everyone. It is similar to apartment living. Advantages are that you own your own unit and the exterior maintenance is taken care of for you. This can be appealing to the elderly, as well as to working singles and couples.

Because of overbuilding in many areas of the country, there are exceptional opportunities in condominiums. When this market surplus is absorbed you can expect excellent appreciation in value.

In purchasing a condominium you should consider the amenities included, as well as association fees. Association fees should be considered as part of your ownership cost. However, these fees are often less than the exterior and ground maintenance expenses associated with single-family home ownership.

Condominiums are frequently promoted as vacation homes. They are desirable in that the owner does not have the responsibility of maintenance, and all the amenities—such as a pool and tennis—are available upon arrival.

YOUR HOME AS AN INVESTMENT

Condominiums make good rental units. Condominium management firms often provide rental services and management for owners.

Be aware, though, that there are growing restrictions in the Midwest and in Florida being placed upon condominium owners with respect to the leasing of condo units; many condo owners who occupy their units have an "anti-investor" bias — possibly with good reason, since not all condo renters maintain the units as well as their owner-neighbors might like. Be sure to investigate attitudes and restrictions in any area where you are considering purchasing a condominium for rent. We recommend that you consult a knowledgeable real estate attorney.

While the terms *cooperative* and *condominium* are often used interchangeably, they refer to different things. A condominium is a vertical subdivision in which an owner owns his or her air space, but owns the common areas, including the land, in common with the other owners. In a cooperative, the property is owned by a corporation and owners have shares in the corporation. Each shareholder has lease rights from the corporation as to the occupancy of a specified unit. While condominiums can be freely transferred, cooperatives generally require that the governing body approve assignments of leases. This tends to restrict transferability.

YOUR HOME AS AN INVESTMENT

VACATION HOMES

A vacation home-purchase is normally an emotional one that is not based on economic considerations. If a vacation home increases your enjoyment of life, it is going to be a wise purchase. If it is a wise investment as well, it is an even wiser purchase.

The bargain vacation home is likely not to be a bargain. As an example, an off-water home in a water-oriented vacation area might be purchased at a great deal less than waterfront property. But the waterfront property is likely to show the greatest appreciation in value.

Vacation homes that have appreciated the greatest in value have been those in the areas of strongest demand. With shorter work weeks and greater disposable income, we can expect future demand to increase the value of vacation homes.

You cannot depreciate your residence. The same holds true for a vacation home if you live in it more than fourteen days a year. By living in a vacation home for fourteen days or less and using it primarily as a rental unit, you can retain the depreciation advantage. If you live in a vacation home more than fourteen days, you can still reduce your cost of ownership by renting it when you are not using it.

YOUR HOME AS AN INVESTMENT

Time shares

Time shares are interval ownerships, usually of resort-type property. The buyer obtains the right to occupy the unit during specific periods each year. Some time shares are fee ownership, which means they go on forever and can be inherited. Other time shares are more like a lease arrangement in that they are for a designated number of years.

Because of extremely high promotion and sales costs, the units sell for a great deal more than the proportionate share of the value of a unit. As an example, a unit sold as a condominium might have a market value of $80,000. If the same unit were to be sold as time shares, fifty weeks might be sold at an average price of $8,000 per week. The gross sales price, instead of being $80,000, would now be $400,000.

Time shares should be considered an investment. Few have ever appreciated in value. Generally, resales have proven difficult and even then they are usually sold at discounts from their original prices.

Don't buy time shares because of exchange privileges to exotic places. The exchange agreements are generally not guaranteed. When all units are sold, it is doubtful that an owner of an undesirable week in one time share will be able to exchange it for a desirable week in another time share.

Time shares, while not an investment, are great for what they are purported to be: a guaranteed vacation home for a specific period each year. (Keep in mind that taxes, maintenance, and owner association fees must also be paid.)

RETIREMENT HOMES

If you intend to retire within the next few years and also intend to relocate, you should consider buying your retirement home now.

An advantage of buying early is that you lock in the price. Future price increases might otherwise make your retirement dream house an impossibility.

By owning a rental unit (your retirement home) prior to retirement, you will be able to shelter income in what will likely be your highest income years.

Generally, it is easy to rent property in retirement-oriented communities. Retirees make excellent tenants. They usually pay rent promptly and maintain the premises.

YOUR HOME AS AN INVESTMENT

HOME AND ACREAGE

A home on a few acres within commuting distance can often be purchased at a price which is competitive with similar housing on a city lot. Having acreage, however, offers more than just the quality of life found in a rural environment. It also offers exceptional investment opportunities. Increasing interest in this type of property can be expected to increase values. In addition, there is also the possibility of future lot splits or subdividing.

Before you purchase a home with acreage you would be wise to check with the county planning department as to what they envision for the area. Ask also about any restrictions on lot splits. If you were considering two such properties, you should give greater consideration to the property where division is likely to be allowed, rather than to the property where division is unlikely to be possible.

GRANNY FLATS

It is often possible to convert existing space in a single-family home to a rental unit. These units are known by a variety of names, including Granny Flats. Basement units are often called English Apartments.

YOUR HOME AS AN INVESTMENT

The conversion of space for rental purposes can be costly. The rents must justify the return. Because the cost might not be recoverable upon resale, it is recommended that converting space to a rental in a single-family home not be undertaken unless the income will recover the costs involved within five years.

SHARING YOUR HOME

Most people don't like the thought of renting a room to a stranger, but renting one or more rooms can make a significant economic difference in the quality of housing you can afford, and even in your ability to own a home.

Homes that are particularly adaptable to room rentals are those offering convenient access to a private or shared bath. Homes close to hospitals and colleges have little difficulty attracting roomers. High apartment rents, as well as the availability of housing, allow comparatively high monthly rents. Some owners rent a room for single occupancy at one rate but charge about 50 percent more for double occupancy. By checking your local papers you will likely be surprised at rental rates for rooms.

When you rent part of your home you are entitled to depreciate the percentage rented. This can mean a significant tax benefit to the owner.

YOUR HOME AS AN INVESTMENT

Single owners will often share their home with another single. Homes that have a bath for both residents are especially adaptable for this type of arrangement. The rental rate for a shared home usually approaches that of a one-bedroom apartment. Besides rent, the renter often pays half of the utilities. Shared housing arrangements such as this can often mean the difference between having a home or having it foreclosed.

BUILD—MOVE IN—SELL

In a good sales market it is possible to sell a home for more than the cost of a lot plus construction. In other words, there is a profit margin possible in building for resale.

Be advised, though, that home construction brings with it a variety of costs that may not be immediately apparent, including title expenses, taxes, and insurances.

Many small builders build a house on speculation, move in when it is completed, and put the house up for sale. They reduce their risk to a minimum. Because they need housing anyway, they can afford to hold the house until they obtain a favorable price.

Many individuals have made significant profits by doing the same thing. They either contract the construction to a general contractor or act as their own general contractor. They move in, landscape, and decorate. Having a good decorator sense as well as fine furniture can make a difference in the sale price, because most buyers buy as much from emotion as they do from logic.

If you wish to use this technique you should plan on putting a large part of any profit into your next better-quality home. A much greater percentage of profit is possible on a $200,000 home than on a $75,000 home. While this gypsy life is not for everyone, for many it has been a pathway to financial security.

TAXES AND HOME OWNERSHIP

The government likes homeowners. Homeowners are responsible citizens who provide stability to the country. Government tax policies encourage home ownership.

While you cannot depreciate your residence for tax purposes, property taxes and interest on your home loan are deductible expenses. These deductions serve to reduce the true cost of home ownership.

Assume a homeowner makes a monthly payment of $1,000, which includes interest, principal, insurance, and taxes. On a new amortized loan, at least $900 of this payment would be for interest and property taxes. If the homeowner were in the

YOUR HOME AS AN INVESTMENT

33 percent tax bracket with a taxable income of $47,000 then the deductibility of the $900 each month would mean a reduction in taxes of $300. The cost of ownership, instead of being $1,000, would be only $700. Therefore, if a taxpayer in the 33 percent bracket could afford $700 per month to *rent* a house, that same taxpayer could afford to *buy* it with a $1,000 payment.

Defer capital gains

Another tax advantage of home ownership is the ability to defer capital gains taxes on profit realized from a sale.

If a new principal residence is purchased within two years of the sale of a principal residence, and the new residence costs the same or more than the sale price of the former residence, then the capital gains can be deferred.

By moving up in housing, you can continue to defer capital gains. At age 55, you can sell without repurchase and have a $125,000 exemption from capital gains taxation.

$125,000 capital gains exemption

Our tax laws provide for a one-time tax-free sale of a residence with a gain of up to $125,000. To qualify, the taxpayer must have lived in the house three of the preceding five years, and at least one spouse must be age 55 or older.

YOUR HOME AS AN INVESTMENT

This exemption makes home ownership even more attractive as the basis for a real estate investment program.

If a person were approaching 55 and wished to sell, they should consider a lease with an option to buy which can only be exercised after they reach age 55. Requiring a large payment for the option would act to ensure that it would be exercised.

THE BEST-RATED RENTAL PROPERTIES

SHOULD YOU BE A LANDLORD?

Before you rush out to buy rental property, you should consider the management aspect. Do you have the time and/or temperament to be a landlord? Many people are not temperamentally suited to deal directly with tenants and their problems. They allow problems to upset them. They don't want to hear complaints. Others don't have the time to manage or the time and/or ability to make repairs. Such persons should either consider management-free real property investments, or professional management.

Though professional management can take a great burden from an owner, it does reduce the owner's net income. Management fees vary based upon area and type of property, but you should expect fees to range from 5 percent to 10 percent of the gross. Professional management generally makes economic sense on large properties but owners of small investment properties can often do a better job of management. A single vacancy for an owner of a duplex would be a priority item, but to a large management firm it would be just one of many problems to be solved.

BEST-RATED RENTAL PROPERTIES

UNECONOMIC DECISION-MAKING

People often hold on to investment property for reasons that are not economic. They may hold on because they don't want to realize a loss or simply because the easiest decision to make is no decision at all. If you would not invest today in a property you presently own at the price you could realize from a sale, then you should seriously consider selling the property and placing the proceeds in a property in which you *would* invest. By keeping the property you are really bidding against others by saying, "I will pay more for the property than you will."

RESIDENTIAL RENTAL PROPERTY

Residential property is the best investment in rental property for many investors. Residential property offers the highest loan-to-value loans at the lowest interest rates. Residential property has the largest number of potential renters so it is relatively easy to rent. Because there are so many residential properties on the market, properties can generally be located which are attractively priced, and often with below-market seller financing.

Single-family rentals

An advantage of buying homes for rental is that purchases can usually be made with little or no down payment. They are readily rentable, having the lowest vacancy rate for all housing. In inflationary periods, single-family homes show great appreciation through refinancing, which creates cash for further investments.

Disadvantages of single-family homes include the fact that rent usually is not sufficient to cover loan payments, taxes, insurance, and maintenance, although positive cash flows are likely to be found in marginal or substandard housing. As rents increase, negative cash flow should disappear.

Single-family homes require more maintenance per rental unit than multifamily dwellings. Maintenance problems can be reduced by leases requiring the tenant to handle or maintain and repair, with exceptions such as the roof, heating, and air conditioning.

The best single-family rentals will be those that can be expected to realize the greatest appreciation. Therefore, choose a rental home using the same economic criteria you would use to choose a residence for yourself.

Condominiums

Like single-family homes, condominiums make excellent rental units. They have an advantage over single-family homes in that the grounds and exterior maintenance are handled by the owners' association. In areas with a condominium glut, condominiums can be purchased with relatively low negative cash flows.

Mobile home rentals

Older single-wide mobile home units that are not in a park have little market value. They can usually be purchased from prices ranging from $2,000 to $5,000. Dealers who have taken such units in trade are often willing to handle the financing themselves with little or no down payment.

These older coaches offer an exceptional rental opportunity if a park can be located that will accept them at a reasonable space fee. Normally, the only parks which will accept older single-wide rental units and have available space are very small parks located in less desirable rural areas. Nevertheless, many owners find excellent rental opportunities even in these less desirable parks. Because these units don't require much furniture they are often rented unfurnished at $75 to $100 per month above the park rent. By renting unfurnished the owner has fewer problems and tenants tend to remain longer. In some cases, owners have been able to recoup the cost of a unit in as little as two years.

Before going into this type of rental, the investor should be prepared for rent collection problems and damage to units, as well as problems with park management.

Apartments

High land and construction costs have made apartment rentals the only choice for many. Besides those who feel they have no housing alternative, apartments are the preferred housing of many. People who are likely to be transferred and those who don't have the time or inclination to bother with the many responsibilities of home ownership prefer apartments.

Apartments have attracted many investors recently. While other real estate values were relatively flat between 1980–1985, rentals in many areas increased at 10 percent per year. This resulted in apartment values soaring in an otherwise lackluster period.

Because sale prices are usually based on rents, the best apartment investments are generally those where current rents can be increased. Rent increases can result in an immediate increase in an owner's equity.

In evaluating rental rates you should not be concerned with what others are renting their units for. What you want to evaluate are vacant units. You would do well to raise rents 5 to 10 percent above similar vacant units, since the cost and bother of relocation will offest slight rent savings possible. To keep tenants satisfied, many land-owners will schedule improvements or repairs at the same time rent is increased.

The most desirable properties are those likely to allow the greatest percentage increases in rent revenues, as well as those that have the greatest appreciation. Rent-controlled properties should be avoided unless they show a reasonable positive cash flow and have provisions for increases in future rent which will cover future increases in the cost of ownership.

Furnished units

Generally, furnished units have a greater turn-over than unfurnished units. This results in a higher vacancy factor as well as higher mainte-nance and management costs.

Nevertheless, one of the better investments can be to buy unfurnished units and furnish them. Furnished units can be rented for significantly higher rates than unfurnished units in many areas. Excellent locations to consider for furnishing units are areas close to colleges, hospitals, airports, or in the central city area. These are usually the high-demand areas for furnished rentals.

By buying apartments at prices based on unfurnished rentals it is possible to furnish them and develop an exceptional positive income, as well as increase the resale value of the property.

BEST-RATED RENTAL PROPERTIES

SUBSTANDARD HOUSING

Before you buy substandard housing you should consider the negative aspects of owning this type of property. You can expect collection problems, tenant damage, vandalism, high insurance costs, high maintenance expense, as well as having to deal with the city regarding tenant complaints.

An advantage of substandard housing is that many investors are not interested. Because of problems, an owner is likely to be highly motivated when he wishes to sell substandard housing. Positive cash flows and minimum down payments are therefore possible.

If there is any secret to successful investments in marginal housing it is management and careful tenant selection. An owner must be willing to make repairs and solve or avoid problems.

ROOMING HOUSES

Rooming houses can be headache properties. High repair and utility costs, rent collection problems, problems between tenants, and dealing with the city regarding code violations tend to turn off most investors. Because of the limited demand, rooming houses, like other substandard housing, can be purchased at attractive prices and terms.

The difference between a successful rental investment and a nightmare is in finding the right manager. You want an elderly person or couple who are healthy and honest—nondrinkers who are on a minimum pension. Often all that are required for reimbursement are free housing, utilities, and dignified treatment.

CONVERSION POSSIBILITIES

Apartment buildings that physically lend themselves to conversion to separately owned condominium or cooperative units deserve your investigation. Buying a 24-unit structure for $600,000 and selling the units at $50,000 each would mean a gross profit of $600,000 (100 percent). If the building had been purchased at 10 percent down, the $60,000 down payment would show a gross profit of 1,000 percent on the investment. Many condominium conversions have shown returns comparable to the example given.

Be sure to check with your local planning commission for any reasons why conversion would not be possible. When evaluating the economics of conversion, check with a civil engineering firm that handles conversions, and ask about cost. For a fee, some firms will handle the engineering and all of the paperwork.

Mansions

Huge old homes are not as desirable as single-family homes because of maintenance and utility

… Depending upon zoning, conversion to other uses should be considered. Common alternative residential uses include apartments, rooming houses, and even nursing homes.

Nursing homes might require expensive fire suppression systems, fire escapes, and a commercial kitchen. Apartments also require extensive plumbing. Another use to consider is a bed-and-breakfast conversion.

There is an increasing interest in these guest houses, both as unique places to stay while traveling, as well as from a business viewpoint by retirees who desire the lifestyle and income of an inn keeper.

Another use of mansions involves conversion to offices. Because of the distinctive nature of old homes it has become fashionable for lawyers, architects, accountants, and other business people to seek the image of strength and stability these structures project. In many areas they command rents normally associated with newer office structures.

Lofts

High ceilings and exposed ducts and pipes appeal to more than just artists; warehouse and factory space can be economically converted to loft rental residences, one of the hottest aspects of the present real estate market. Normally, the owner simply partitions the space into large areas and provides each with electrical outlets, a bath, and a kitchen. In some cases, new elevators are installed. The space can also be sold as condominium lofts, with or without improvements.

Be warned, though, that zoning requirements pertaining to such conversions can be strict, and that the cost of improvements necessary to meet those requirements can render a loft-conversion investment infeasible.

OFFICE BUILDINGS

The distinctive structures offering great pride of ownership are generally not the best investment for owners seeking income.Pride-of-ownership properties offer appreciation possibilities because they are in demand, but it is likely to take many years before the income justifies the investment.

The best buys in office buildings are generally class C structures close to a city's central area. Class C are the oldest, least desirable office buildings. They can frequently be purchased for little more than land value. These buildings usually have high turnover rates and the least desirable tenants. Inexperienced investors should be wary of making such an investment, unless in the context of a Real Estate Investment Trust or Real Estate Limited Partnership.

BEST-RATED RENTAL PROPERTIES

The reason why class C office buildings can be the best investment is that the space can usually be renovated to desirable class B-type space at less than 25 percent of the cost of a new structure. Class B space is found in older, reasonably modern buildings that are well-maintained. Because of the low capital investment, rents in renovated office buildings can be set attractively so they will insure full occupancy and still provide an exceptional return on the investment.

Class A buildings in trouble can be excellent investments. Class A buildings are the newest, most desirable office buildings. Because of high vacancy rates, many such structures have been foreclosed and are available from the lenders at significant savings. Keep in mind, however, that a bargain you cannot rent is not a bargain at any price.

COMMERCIAL AND INDUSTRIAL PROPERTY

The best buys in commercial and industrial property are in problem properties having severe vacancy problems. Your ability to solve the problems determines if the investment is a wise choice. You must be able to either convert problem property to other uses or find tenants for it; otherwise you will be the owner of the problem.

BEST-RATED RENTAL PROPERTIES

Mini-warehouses

In many areas mini-warehouses are providing exceptional returns. They can be built on leased land to reduce investments. Many owners of expensive sites have developed mini-warehouses as a temporary use which allows them to hold the land for greater appreciation.

Similar to mini-warehouse use are storage yards for recreational vehicles. Land ownership is not necessary as owners holding land for future development are interested in a land lease, which reduces their costs of holding the property.

Mobile home parks

Mobile home parks are a very attractive investment. One reason is that mobile homes on rented sites in better parks are not really mobile. Tenants generally have a great deal of money invested in setting double- and triple-wide units on the site, in site improvements, and in cabanas and car ports. The cost to move a unit and duplicate its amenities in another park could be in excess of $10,000.

Once a new park is filled there are very few units moved. The vacancy factor inherent in other rental properties does not significantly exist. Rent increases must be paid by the tenant or they must bear the cost of moving the mobile home. Because of the extremely strong position of park owners, many areas have enacted rent control and other statutes protecting park residents. Rent control or its likelihood would negatively effect the sale price of mobile home parks.

Generally, filled mobile home parks require significant down payments in order to obtain a positive cash flow. It is common for new owners to raise rents upon purchase so that a positive cash flow can be obtained with a more modest down payment.

Mobile home parks that have below-market rents or are otherwise not operating up to potential can be especially attractive investments.

Because of the great interest in mobile home parks, some developers buy or obtain options on land, obtain zoning changes if needed, and get approvals for mobile home parks. They then sell the package to developers.

Because mobile homes are not truly mobile, a mobile home park that can be sold off as condominiums offers great potential for capital gains. If the statutes and planning commission will allow condominium conversion, the likely buyers for the spaces will be the former renters. The high costs associated with moving and setting up large mobile homes will literally force park residents to buy their spaces.

BEST-RATED RENTAL PROPERTIES

Recreational vehicle parks

The basic differences between mobile home parks and recreational vehicle parks are the size of the spaces and term of the rental.

More units are possible per acre when renting to the smaller recreational vehicle. Because these units are truly mobile, the spaces are often rented on a daily basis, although some desirable resort area parks require rental by the month or season.

Some recreational vehicle parks, like mobile home parks, are developed for sale of individual spaces, or sell club memberships which allow use of space in a number of parks.

The success in purchasing or developing a recreational vehicle park is related to location. A good park in a prime location will show phenomenal results.

Resorts

Older seasonal resorts are often available at a relatively low cost per unit. A few months' operation as a resort cannot show an income to justify a high price. If the units can be subdivided so they can be separately sold, or if they can be sold as condominiums, an exceptional profit is possible. In many areas of the country the prices of older resorts have been driven up, largely because of competition between developers.

THE BEST-RATED LAND INVESTMENTS

NONAGRICULTURAL LAND

Nonagricultural land values are related to the likelihood of future benefits, specifically, the likelihood of development.

While land values might remain static for years, a major construction boom can cause values of land offering development potential to soar. Appreciation in value of 1,000 percent in just a few years has not been unusual.

Raw nonagricultural land is a negative cash flow investment. Even when there is no debt there are still taxes to be paid. Because holding land for appreciation costs money, sellers are often anxious to be relieved of the financial burden. It is common for sellers to finance buyers with little or no down payment and give below market-rate seller financing as well.

Because of our tax laws, land investments are particularly attractive to those in the highest tax brackets. Interest is a deductible expense. If a person is in the 25 percent tax bracket, paying 10 percent interest would really only amount to a net interest of 7½ percent, because Uncle Sam pays the rest by the deduction. However, for a person in the 50 percent tax bracket, 10 percent interest is reduced to a net cost of 5 percent because of the deductibility of interest from taxable income.

A disadvantage of land investments is that, unlike other real estate investments, there is no depreciation. Improvements can be depreciated but land cannot.

Another disadvantage of land as an investment is that it is difficult to borrow on. Few lenders will make loans on undeveloped land. Those who will demand high interest.

FARMLAND

The near catastrophic drop in farm prices over the past few years has created some unusual opportunities for investors. While the drop in value of prime farmland has been leveling off, marginal farmland prices are still declining. It is likely that marginal land will continue to be taken out of production.

At one time gentleman farmers purchased farmland primarily for the tax benefits of depreciation on the improvements, as well as for pride of ownership. Today's farm prices make income a prime factor in investment. In many areas of the country prime farmland can be purchased at prices which will yield a 5 to 10 percent return. An additional consideration is appreciation. Many economists feel that prime farmland prices will rebound after the wave of panic selling and foreclosures that resulted from disastrously high interest rates and low grain prices.

When grain prices were high, a great deal of marginal land was put into production. This land cannot support the high costs of farming. The reduction in acreage because of marginal land being no longer farmed can be expected to firm up grain prices as well as increase land values for prime farmland.

Farm investments are not for everyone. Buyers should be in a high tax bracket to take maximum benefit of depreciation. They should understand that commodity price changes and weather can result in an operational loss. Even when the farm is leased, a loss by the operator might mean an inability to pay the rent. For those investors who can handle farm investments the best recommendation would be prime cropland (not grain) of 400 acres or more. The land can be leased or placed under professional management. There are many local and regional management farm companies, some specializing in particular aspects of agriculture.

Some investors are buying farms and leasing them to farmers, giving the lessee an option to purchase after a period of years. They thus obtain income, depreciation, and a set appreciation if the option is exercised. Since most farmers want to buy, the option helps to ensure that the farm will be well maintained. In many cases the lessee is the original owner who lost the farm because of inability to service the debt.

Limited partnerships also buy farms for leasing to operators for rent. This increased investor interest in farms will help the recovery of farm prices.

If you are interested in farms as investments you should check lenders in farm areas. While they normally won't indicate which farmers are in difficulty, they will tell you about farmers who might consider selling. (These will be the ones in financial difficulty.) Some investors have been able to purchase farms in these distress cases by curing the financial delinquencies and assuming or refinancing the debt, while leasing back to the former owner with a right to repurchase. Everyone benefits by an arrangement such as this. The farmer can remain on the farm and has the opportunity to regain ownership, and the investor obtains depreciation, income, and appreciation opportunities.

If you are not knowledgeable about farming you should consider professional help before buying. There are a number of agricultural consultants who can help you in evaluating investment farms.

BEST-RATED LAND INVESTMENTS

SCENIC FARMLAND

Most of the really scenic farmland is marginal farmland. While hills and woods don't lend themselves to farming, there is opportunity in this type of marginal farmland. Prices for this type of land has fallen drastically.

Such farms within about a 90-minute drive from metropolitan areas can be good investments, but not for farming. The subdivision of these farms into smaller acreage parcels can result in significant increase in value. There is a large demand for these sites for hobby farms, vacation or retirement homes, and even camping sites. These farms can often be divided with minimum engineering expense and improvements. Before purchasing a farm for this purpose you should check with your county planning commission to inquire about subdivision restrictions or requirements. You should also check with a civil engineering firm to get estimated costs.

DESOLATE LAND

Land that is far removed from cities, has little scenic beauty, and is not productive for mining or agriculture can be purchased at extremely low prices and fantastic terms.

However, the appreciation in value of such land is unlikely to exceed the rate of inflation. Such land should be avoided even at what may appear to be a bargain price. Land is not a bargain at any price if no one else will want it.

PARCEL SIZE

The principle that smaller can be better often applies when considering land investments. Generally, the smaller a parcel of land, the higher the price per acre. The reason for this is simple supply-and-demand economics. There are more investors interested in small parcels than in large parcels. Therefore, the price of smaller parcels tends to be bid higher by the market demand.

Because of this fact, you can often increase your equity by simply splitting a parcel of land into two or more pieces. Therefore, parcels that can be easily split would be better investments than parcels that cannot be split, or that might be difficult to split.

LOTS

Lots are a management-free investment. Other than paying the taxes and any mortgage payments, the investor simply waits until he or she is ready to sell or develop the land.

Commercial lots can be excellent investments. While they sell at a great deal more than residential lots, the appreciation can be much greater. Because of appreciation in value, commercial lot owners are often able to use their equity to finance major development.

In snow areas, lot sales tend to slow down in November; the activity starts up again in late February. The best time to buy in these areas would be in December, when there are fewest buyers.

Generally, the lots in the first phase of a large development sell for much less than later phases. Low prices are often used to create interest. When the first phase is sold out, prices generally are increased for later phases. The price increases are likely to be greatest in industrial and commercial developments. An even greater advantage is possible by agreeing to purchase in the first phase prior to completion of the development work. A subdivider will often take a lower price for an early commitment because it will reduce the risks of the development. Further, presales help to increase interest in the development.

For sale signs on lots don't always mean the seller really wants to sell. They are often placed by "Will Sell" sellers who want to test the market more than they want to sell. Because of the low expense of holding onto paid-for lots, you will find many "Will Sell" owners. They usually will sell only if they can get a premium price that exceeds market value.

BEST-RATED LAND INVESTMENTS

LAND RESEARCH

Before investing in land for appreciation you should visit your city or county planning office. They will likely have projections for the growth and use of the land.

By checking on zoning changes, you will be able to spot areas where zoning is likely to be changed to more favorable uses. A change in zoning could have a significant effect on value.

Never put an offer on land contingent upon a favorable zoning change. This would simply serve to give the owner your idea. It would be better to obtain an option to purchase and then apply for a zoning change.

County and state highway departments can be contacted about anticipated future roads, as well as anticipated changes to the existing system. Changes could target areas that will likely have the greatest appreciation.

By checking county records you can determine who has been buying land and where. This can lead you to areas likely to have the greatest appreciation. For instance, when a factory buys land it indicates the intent to use it for manufacturing or warehousing facilities. Even if the present zoning does not fit these uses, buying land in the same vicinity can be an astute action, since zoning change is likely.

BEST-RATED LAND INVESTMENTS

When one person or firm is buying a great number of parcels or a very large parcel it could be wise to make a purchase or obtain an option to buy within the area. Such activity usually means the land is being assembled for a development purpose. A large development increases the value of undeveloped property around it.

OPTIONS

When making a land purchase, it is relatively easy to obtain an option to any additional land owned by the seller. Your offer to purchase should include the option. It shouldn't be necessary to offer additional consideration for the option. In effect, what you will get is an option to buy more land at a definite price for a definite period of time. You want the period to be as long as possible. If the value of land increases during the option period you would then sell either the land or the option.

LAND COMPANIES

There are many firms which buy huge parcels of land, break them into small parcels, and tout them as investment properties with heavy promotion. The markup over land costs added by these companies is often in the 1,000 percent range. Fantastic appreciation would be required before a parcel would ever be worth what the investor paid.

These are really premature subdivisions which will hurt the eventual development of the area because of the inability of future developers to put together large parcels.

You should be wary of buying from land companies that heavily promote their product or use high-pressure sales tactics. If you like an area being promoted, you should contact local real estate brokers. By avoiding promotional sellers you will be able to buy land without paying a premium price.

THE BEST-RATED LIMITED PARTNERSHIPS

HOW PARTNERSHIPS WORK

A Real Estate Limited Partnership (RELP) is a partnership where the investor, the *limited partner,* has limited liability. The limited partner supplies money only and has no liability beyond his or her investment. Some partnerships are public, while others are private.

The operating partner is called the *general partner.* The general partner normally puts the partnership together, finding investors and property. The general partner is normally a corporation. In a limited partnership you are paying for the professional management of your general partner.

A major advantage that RELPs have over corporations is that the depreciation from the property purchased is passed directly through to the investors, which can mean a significant tax shelter.

Different RELPs have different goals. Some are structured for maximum income while others are organized to provide the greatest tax shelter and/or appreciation. Some RELPs invest in a particular type of property while others take a broad approach to investing.

BEST-RATED RELPs

Public partnerships

Some public partnerships are often sold on a nationwide basis through stock brokers. Others are sold direct by the general partner, who is able to raise huge amounts in order to buy and/or develop large investment properties such as shopping malls and industrial parks. An advantage of investing in a RELP is that it allows a small investor to participate in quality investments.

Public partnerships are usually blind pools in that properties are not purchased or developed until all the money is in. The investor may know in general how the money will be invested but the specific properties have not been chosen. Public RELPs have sales costs and fees; not every dollar invested is available to purchase or develop real property. Because of competition, costs and fees have in many cases dropped to 13 percent or less, which means that at least 87 cents of every dollar should be available for investment. Limited partnerships where less than 87 percent is available for investment should generally be avoided.

The general partner is paid a percentage of the cash flow for management. Upon sale, the general partner customarily receives a percentage of the profit after the investment of the partners is repaid. This profit percentage could be in the 20 percent range and is an inducement for the general partner to sell at a profit rather than to hold for the management fees.

BEST-RATED RELPs

Private partnerships

Private partnerships are local interstate partnerships with just a handful of investors. State law determines the maximum number of partners. Such partnerships are usually put together to buy a particular property.

Private partnerships normally require a significant investment, such as $25,000. Investments in public partnerships do not need to be as large. Many will accept investments as low as $2,000, encouraging people to invest using their IRA accounts.

In private partnerships the general partner is often a fellow investor. More of the investment is available for purchase or development since many general partners of private partnerships take no fees up front. They do, however, take a management percentage and a percentage of the profit.

Payouts

General partners normally try to close out a RELP within 8 to 10 years. Having a track record of income, tax benefits, and profits attracts investors for the next partnership. Many general partners are constantly setting up new partnerships.

When properties are sold, the money is distributed to the investors, who pay capital gains tax on their profit. With syndicates that have invested in a number of properties, the sales could be spread over a number of years, with profits distributed with each sale.

In the past, limited partnerships that had greatly appreciated in value were frequently refinanced. This allowed the return of the investment to the limited partnership without a sale. You should not count on this type of appreciation for the future. You can probably expect future appreciation to exceed the cost of living by about 4 percent annually.

Even though a partnership is closed out, the investors might not obtain all their profits upon sale. Partnerships often have to carry paper, causing the payoff to be spread over a long period of time.

Another drawback of RELPs is that an investor would likely have a difficult time selling his or her interest if a sale were necessary.

The relatively new National Partnership Exchange (NAPEX) offers greater liquidity for some RELPs. The computerized service of NAPEX creates a competitive auction process in which a sale listing is posted and members have seven days to bid for the listing. After the bidding process, the seller can accept or reject the highest bid. Generally, recently formed RELPs sell at a significant discount from offering prices. The properties in these RELPs would not have appreciated enough to cover all of the original sales costs associated with organizing the limited partnerships. While NAPEX plans to expand, they presently deal only in approximately 65 major RELPs. They have about 14,000 registered representatives, including major stock brokerage firms. Besides functioning as a source to sell RELPs, NAPEX offers a fine opportunity to buy shares in quality limited partnerships at a discounted price. NAPEX also publishes a year-end price list and previous transactions guide describing what shares are being traded. If your broker is not familiar with NAPEX have him or her call 1-800-356-2739.

Liquidity Fund Investment Corporation, 1900 Powell Street, Suite 235, Emeryville, CA 94608-1831 is one of a growing number of firms that will buy your RELP interest if you must liquidate. These firms usually want partnerships that are several years old, and that have presumably appreciated in value; discounts in the 20 to 35 percent range are likely. RELPs offering good cash returns are the easiest to sell.

Major stockbrokers will also help you sell your RELP interest. Remember that, because of the sales difficulties and discounts, RELPs are not for everyone. If you are nearing retirement, for instance, don't become a limited partner. The payoff date is too uncertain.

If your marriage is not stable, avoid a RELP. Divorce could necessitate a sale that could mean a substantial loss.

If you are carrying inadequate life insurance you might not want to become a limited partner. If you should die before the partnership is dissolved, your survivors might be in a position where they would have to sell at a loss. Similarly, if your income or job is not secure, a RELP might not be for you. You don't want to be in a position where you are forced to liquidate.

If you will need money at some specific time to send children to college, or for any other major need, don't invest in a RELP. It may not have liquidated by the time you need the money.

LEVERAGE

Some highly leveraged RELPs (high debt-to-investment ratio) were in trouble in the early 1980s because of high interest and a slow economy. Many properties were foreclosed.

While a high-leveraged position allows an investor great depreciation and appreciation advantages, a highly leveraged investment requires high rents and occupancy rates. Otherwise, a negative cash flow situation will exist. Today, limited partnerships are using more cash and less borrowed capital to protect their investors against negative market changes.

If there is a recession or a low level of inflation, limited partnerships which use no or low leverage would be the best investments. They would provide security and a positive cash flow. Unleveraged partnerships are an alternative to bonds as far as safety goes, and also provide appreciation possibilities. The yield on quality low- and no-leverage RELPs is competitive with treasury bond yields. Low- or no-leveraged partnerships are excellent investments for IRA accounts where safety is of primary concern.

During an inflationary period, highly leveraged partnerships would provide the greatest appreciation per dollar of investment. Keep in mind that risk increases proportionally as leverage is increased.

INVESTIGATE BEFORE YOU INVEST

Public RELPs will supply you with colorful brochures about the general partner and past performance. They may also provide a heavy prospectus on a current offering. Good general partners are generous with data and will respond to specific questions.

Consider the past track record of a general partner. You don't want to be the one who is paying for a general partner's education in a first partnership.

You are interested in the profit made on those partnerships which have sold out, as well as present cash returns on current limited partnerships. Pay particular attention to the income from limited partnerships formed since 1980, since they probably reflect what you can expect in a few years. Don't pay too much attention to statements about value increases of property that has not been sold. Those estimates are likely to be on the high side.

Keep in mind that during the 1970s just about all real estate enjoyed increases in value. Don't count on that type of appreciation in the future.

Unfortunately, some general partners will sell properties that have appreciated in value and hold on to those with little or no appreciation. From the information provided, the partnership may appear to be performing well when in fact it may be performing marginally. Be wary of RELPs that have sold half or more of their properties, but that have seen no sales activity for two or three years. This could indicate the situation described above.

Partnerships which seem to be selling more of a tax shelter than an investment are suspect. Tax shelters that appear too good to be true probably are not. Claims of write-offs in excess of the dol-

BEST-RATED RELPs

lars you invest in the year of investment might excite many investors but are also likely to alert the attention of the IRS. You don't want to be buying a tax audit and disallowance of your shelter.

You should consider that RELPs which develop property run the risk of cost overruns. You, therefore, do not want too much leverage in a RELP that will be in development. You also want a general partner who has pertinent development experience. Keep in mind that while development provides new structures with lower maintenance, development partnerships also produce an unproven property with no income record.

Is your initial investment your total investment? Some RELPs call for a series of investments. There can be tax benefits in doing this, but if your income fluctuates you might not be able to meet your commitments.

The written material supplied by the general partner will probably list investors in other limited partnerships. If a similar RELP has had a number of pension-plan investors, you can probably assume a low risk factor; pension plans research their investments and look for safe and well-managed RELPs.

When you check the various partnerships you will see that they compute yields in different ways, which makes comparisons difficult even for accountants. The footnotes tend to confuse rather than clarify. Some RELPs will show yields based on dollars paid and not on what the partners paid. This will overstate the profit. Others will show yields, but the yield might include that portion retained by the general partner and would not show the investors' yield.

Your stockbroker will be happy to recommend RELPs. While you should consider your broker's advice, don't accept it blindly. Some brokerage firms are exclusive sales agents for RELPs; other brokerage firms have set up their own RELPs. Brokerage company RELPs have not generally shown the level of performance of private general partnerships. A recommendation of such a RELP might mean maximum brokerage commission, but might not be in your best interest.

EVALUATING PRIVATE OFFERINGS

You should evaluate the property that is to be purchased or developed by a private RELP. If it doesn't make sense as an investment you should avoid it.

Investigate the general partner's experience. This is especially important if a property is to be developed. Also investigate the general partner's reputation for integrity. A credit check might also be worthwhile. Don't invest in a private RELP unless you have absolute trust in the general partner.

BEST-RATED RELPs

Ask the general partner for the names and numbers of investors in other partnerships he or she has managed. A few phone calls to these investors could reassure you or help you make the decision to avoid the investment.

Insist on the results of *all* of the partnerships with which the general partner has been involved, not just some of them.

Private partnerships should deal with properties close to the general partner. Be wary of a private partnership that handles investments that are more than an hour's drive from the general partner.

YOUR OWN RELP

Many general partners started out as investors in a private limited partnership. They struck out on their own because they felt that they could do what the general partner did.

To be a successful general partner you must have a good knowledge of the real estate marketplace and be able to evaluate investment property. You must also have the dedication and the time.

Before you rush out and start selling shares, see an attorney. State and federal registration is required of some limited partnerships, but some smaller ones may be exempt. The offerings and contracts must of course comply with the law.

If you are a member of the National Association of Realtors, you should consider becoming involved in the Real Estate Securities and Syndication Institute (RESSI). The institute offers excellent courses as well as professional designations in syndication (a syndication is a partnership).

BEST-RATED RELPs

The following public general partners are recommended based on experience, philosophy, and past performance:

Public Storage, Inc.
900 South Fair Oaks Avenue
P.O. Box 6000
Pasadena, CA 91102
(800) 421-2856

Self-storage and business park developer. Past partnerships have shown a steady increase in income. From 1980 to 1984 rents rose 15.4 percent annually. Land sites are chosen for appreciation. The partnerships are conservatively leveraged. The general partner has a philosophy of a long-term hold for appreciation of the land. No partnerships have been closed out and only one property has been sold. This is a long-term investment for income, safety, and appreciation.

BEST-RATED RELPs

JMB
Sales agent: Merrill Lynch & Company

The general partner has a reputation of professional management and quality properties; primarily shopping centers and office and industrial properties. Conservatively leveraged. You should expect a positive return on your investment (which should increase each year until sale), as well as appreciation and tax benefits.

Krupp Securities Corporation
Harbor Plaza
470 Atlantic Avenue
Boston, MA 02210
(617) 423-2233

The general partner has had a good track record. Their cash-plus limited partnerships are recommended for income, safety, and marketability. These partnerships invest in a combination of insured mortgage securities and quality unleveraged real estate. The cash-plus RELPs are structured so that investors get a Depository Receipt which can be exchanged for a limited partnership interest. The Depository Receipt will have marketability because the partnership will apply for quotation of the Depository Receipts on NASDAQ (National Association of Security Dealers Automated Quotations).

Franchise Finance Corporation of America
Sales agent: E. F. Hutton

The general partner purchases and leases fast-food restaurants. Lessees with less than minimum financing standards must obtain rental insurance. Because the partnerships have been operating without leverage, cash yield should exceed that of government securities. The partnerships should be considered a long-term hold for yield, security, and appreciation.

Jacques-Miller
211 Seventh Avenue, North
Nashville, TN 37219
(800) 251-2003

Jacques-Miller has built an excellent reputation in multifamily properties. The firm renovates its properties to maximize rents. Their partnerships deserve the attention of high-income investors looking for appreciation and tax shelters.

VMS Realty
8700 West Bryn Mawr
Chicago, IL 60631-3504
(Sales Agent: Prudential Bache Securities, Inc.)

A large, experienced syndicator with an excellent past record of limited partnerships. They attempt to target their investments in growth areas. Past investments have been primarily residential, office structures, and hotels. Their current offerings include a mortgage partnership which will finance purchases for their other limited partnerships, as well as Real Estate Investment Trusts.

BEST-RATED RELPs

Wells Investment Securities
  3885 Holcomb Bridge Road
  Norcross, Georgia 30092
  (800) 448-1010

Wells' limited partnerships have developed and purchased Williamsburg-style office buildings in Atlanta and other Southeastern growth cities. The partnerships have been structured for safety and income using cash or conservative leverage. Previous developments have shown an exceptionally high occupancy rate.

None of their partnerships have sold properties. They have, however, shown good cash returns with a high percentage of the return sheltered. Expect a long-term hold. A best buy for income and appreciation.

Realty Income Corporation
  200 West Grand Avenue
  Escondido, CA 92025-2686
  (800) 854-1967

This limited partnership buys triple-net leased property for long-term investments paying cash. The triple-net lease means the tenants pay taxes, insurance, and perform all maintenance. This reduces management responsibility. Many of the purchases are sale-leaseback arrangements. Tenants include regional and national chains and franchises, as well as joint ventures in multitenant structures. The leases provide for cost of living adjustments or adjustments based on tenants' sales volume.

Realty Income Corporation partnerships are structured for income. They do not sell their property. However, their partnerships have shown a strong income which has had an excellent growth rate. This is an excellent investment for an IRA or for anyone who is looking for strong and increasing income.

Lansing Capital Corporation
800 El Camino Real
Menlo Park, CA 94025
(800) 227-8228

The general partner has had an impressive history; the partnership has successfully renovated many older office structures.

The partnership is currently setting up income fund partnerships which make short-term loans taking a participation equity interest, as well as the direct purchase of income property. This type of fund offers high income appreciation as well as an exceptional tax shelter because of depreciation on its own properties, and on participation properties. Upon sale or refinancing, the investors must receive the return of their capital plus a cumulative return of 10 percent per year before the general partner shares in the profits. This type of partnership offers appreciation, and is a best buy for income and as a tax shelter.

THE BEST-RATED REITs

HOW REITs WORK

REITs (pronounced *reets*) are Real Estate Investment Trusts organized under federal law. While they are required to have 75 percent of their assets in real estate, mortgage-backed securities qualify as real estate. If a REIT gives 95 percent of its earnings to the shareholders in the form of dividends, the REIT is not taxed on its earnings. By passing their earnings through to the stockholders, REITs avoid the double taxation of corporations.

REIT interests are similar to shares in a closed-end mutual fund; once the REIT shares have been sold the only way to buy in is to purchase a share from an owner wishing to sell.

Like limited partnerships, a REIT investment allows a small investor the opportunity to take part in quality investments without management responsibility or personal liability beyond his or her investment.

Liquidity

The major advantage a REIT investment has over a limited partnership is ready liquidity.

REITs trade like stocks. Many are listed on the New York Stock Exchange and American Stock Exchange. An investor in a REIT, therefore, does not have the long-term commitment that is part of a limited partnership.

Taxation

Depreciation of a limited partnership is passed directly through to the partners. This is not the case with REITs, which treat depreciation as an expense. Therefore, the reported income of REITs would be less than the actual cash flow. When dividends to shareholders exceed reported earnings, the excess would be a return of capital, which is not taxable to the investor. In some REITs, 50 percent or more of the income has been sheltered.

FREITs

Most REITs have an indefinite life. They buy and hold property or securities. While they are not compelled to sell, they will generally sell when they can no longer depreciate a property. They may reinvest the proceeds or distribute them to the shareholders.

Some REITs set a time period in which they will place their assets on the market. They have a finite rather than an indefinite life. These Finite Real Estate Investment Trusts are known as FREITs.

BEST-RATED REITs

FREITs generally provide that the trustee can extend the dissolution date based upon market conditions. A FREIT might otherwise have to liquidate at an inopportune time.

FREITs are generally priced higher than indefinite-life REITs. The reason for this is that the value of shares in REITs are usually based on income rather than on market value of the assets owned. The stock value is thus usually less than asset value. As dissolution time nears, the value of FREITs goes up based on the expectation of sales above market value of the shares.

REIT PROPERTIES

Most new REITs are blind pools where investors do not know the REIT's exact investments, but only the announced investment strategy, that is, the type of properties to be purchased or developed. Some REITs develop or purchase properties for particular franchises.

Mortgage REITs make loans rather than invest in properties. While mortgage REITs show excellent dividends they are more like bonds than equity REITs. Like bonds, they tend to drop in value as interest rates rise, and increase in value as interest rates fall. Many older mortgage REITs own property because of foreclosures.

BEST-RATED REITs

Some mortgage REITs make large participation loans whereby they take an equity position as well as a creditor position for making the loan. These REITs are likely to show appreciation as well as high income. However, the appreciation in value will not be as great as if they had taken full ownership.

Hybrid REITs are trusts which own property as well as invest in mortgages. While they generally have lower dividends than full-mortgage REITs, they generally show higher dividends than equity REITs. Similarly, they can expect to show greater appreciation than mortgage REITs but less than REITs investing in real property.

PAST PROBLEMS OF REITs

In the early 1970s a number of REITs experienced financial difficulty. They were highly leveraged and were unable to attain sufficient income to cover their debt service.

Today the majority of REITs are using far less leverage. Quite a few are buying for cash. A positive cash flow can, therefore, be shown even with a relatively high vacancy factor and low rents. Most REITs today are considerably safer than stock investments.

BEST-RATED REITs

REITs FOR RETIREMENT AND SAVINGS PLANS

Some stockbrokers might try to dissuade you from investing in REITs through an IRA or other retirement plan. They might suggest various mutual funds instead. You should keep in mind that mutual fund investments generally offer a broker greater commissions, especially if it happens to be a fund managed by his or her own brokerage firm. Since REITs are shares of stock, the broker receives only a normal transaction fee for a REIT investment.

Because the average dividend yield of REITs exceeds the average stock yield, and because equity REITs offer appreciation just as common stock does, you should consider rolling over any stocks held in your IRA to a REIT. For a retirement plan you should consider only REITs with a debt ratio of 50 percent or less to the market value of the properties held. For income and safety many retirement-minded investors prefer mortgage REITs to equity REITs. If you wish to accumulate a nest egg, brokers generally offer a dividend reinvestment program. Your dividends will thus be used to increase your shares in the REIT.

LOCATING THE BEST REITs

Your best investment would be an older REIT that has been showing a steady increase in dividends over a period of years. Besides the security of low debt-to-asset value, these older REITs also have old leases. As these leases expire they are rewritten at market rents, which will increase the future yield.

Another major advantage of older REITs is that they are more likely to be bargains based on market value. By buying into an older REIT you are in effect buying real estate at discount prices. As an example, a REIT might have 10 million shares outstanding and have a price per share of $10. However, the market value of the equity in the property owned might be $150 million, equivalent to $15 per share in asset value. Stock prices of REITs are related more to the specific dividends paid, changes in the dividends, and market conditions than to the underlying shareholders' equity.

Your stockbroker can give you current quotes on REITs, as well as current yields. Ask for a copy of the *Value Line Sheet,* which will give you an excellent evaluation of performance.

An indication that a REIT is an exceptional investment would be to find that management personnel were buying significant numbers of shares for themselves. A number of market newsletters report on insider trading.

Realty Stock Review; 230 Park Avenue; New York, NY, 10169 is an excellent REITs newsletter. It is available for $244 per year, and ranks REITs on terms of past, present, and anticipated performances, as well as by leverage, management, cash flow, and other factors.

You should consider diversifying among a number of quality REITs in the same manner that a stock portfolio would be balanced among various corporations. Diversification would allow income safety should one REIT fail to perform as expected. There is even a mutual fund set up to invest in REITs, the National Securities Real Estate Stock Fund; 605 Third Avenue; New York, NY, 10158.

BEST-RATED REITs

Santa Anita Realty (NYSE-SAR)

While selling close to asset value, this equity REIT has been showing an excellent growth in earnings. The principal asset is the Santa Anita racetrack near Los Angeles, but it also owns half-interest in a one-million square foot mall in which 37 percent of the leases become due in 1989 and 50 percent in the following five years. The REIT also owns neighborhood shopping centers. Increased racing days at Minnesota's Caterbury Downs track is another positive reason we are bullish on SAR for income and appreciation.

BankAmerica Realty (NYSE-BRE)

This is a hybrid REIT with 63 percent of its assets invested in equity properties and 37 percent in mortgages. It has shown an excellent yield. The stock has been selling at a significant discount from market value of its assets. An excellent investment for an IRA because of income and safety.

Lomas & Nettleton Mortgage (NYSE-LOM)

A mortgage trust primarily in higher-interest construction loans. Problem loans are being eliminated and the present high yield is likely to increase, which should be reflected in increased value of its shares. A best buy for income and moderate appreciation.

United Dominion Realty Trust (NASDAQ-UDRT)

This equity trust acquires property for upgrade through capital improvements to maximize income. The trust is leveraged. Refinancing of existing loans at current lower rates offers the possibility of greatly increased earnings. With its better than average management, this trust is a best buy for income and appreciation.

Federal Realty (NYSE-FRT)

This is an equity REIT that invests primarily in older shopping centers, which it renovates and holds for income. It uses funds from its dividend reinvestment program for renovation and new purchases. A best buy for appreciation and future high dividends; current dividends are in the 6 percent range.

New Plan Realty Trust (ASE-NPR)

This trust has shown about a 10 percent increase in earnings each year since 1980. The trust is primarily an equity trust with income-producing residential, commercial, and industrial properties. Additionally, New Plan owns several mortgages from sale of properties. The philosophy is to purchase older property in prime locations for income growth. A best buy for income and appreciation.

Washington R.E.I.T. (ASE-WRE)

The property of this equity trust is located primarily in the Washington, D.C. area. The policy of the trust is to maximize income by improving its property. Its assets are invested about equally in residential properties, office buildings, and shopping centers. Only one of the trust's properties is rent controlled. The trust has increased its dividends every year since 1975. It is a best buy for income and appreciation.

Pennsylvania R.E.I.T. (ASE-PEI)

Besides buying for income, this equity trust also
develops property. The majority of its assets are
in apartments, but it also owns shopping centers
and industrial property. Dividends have shown a
steady and healthy growth. It is a best buy for
income and appreciation.

Property Trust of America (NASDAQ-PTRAS)

An equity trust showing an exceptional high yield.
Sixty percent of its assets are invested in Texas,
primarily in the El Paso area. Only 8 percent is in
office structures, with 43 percent in shopping
centers and 29 percent in apartments. The trust
is in a good cash position for further acquisitions.
While formerly a hybrid trust, it has sold most of
its loan portfolio. The trust is a best buy for
income and appreciation.

BUYING RIGHT

THE BEST TIME TO BUY

The best investments are those where your equity increases on the day of the investment. In other words, property purchased below market value.

When you purchased property at market value, you suffer a loss on the date of purchase. The act of selling property costs money. Commission and sales costs might total 10 percent. Therefore, the property would have to appreciate in value before you could expect to break even on a sale.

You want investments which have a market value *greater* than what you paid. You can find such properties, but you have to look for them and know when you have found them.

A bargain is not necessarily a bargain for you. If you can't make the payments on a bargain purchase, it is not a bargain for you at any price. You should look for properties that meet your individual capabilities and needs.

In every market there are a few excellent opportunities. However, in buyers' markets where there are few purchasers and too many sellers, there are many more opportunities to buy real property below market value.

The reason for buyer's markets is usally high interest rates, which deter most potential buyers from even looking. Motivated sellers tend to become desperate in this type of market.

FINDING A REAL ESTATE AGENT

In searching for investment property you should talk to agents. Real estate fees are customarily paid by sellers, not buyers. A knowledgeable agent knows the market and can make your search more productive.

Let agents know what you are looking for; be completely honest. Some won't be interested in helping you; others will lack the knowledge to meet your needs.

Chances are that you are going to find a knowledgeable agent willing to work with you, and with whom you will develop a rapport. An agent whom you trust and who understands your needs is a valuable ally. Treat such an agent with respect and direct all inquiries about other agents' listings to your own agent. An agent who knows you want to deal only through him or her will work hard to find the investments you seek.

BUYING RIGHT

MOTIVATED SELLERS

Without a motivated seller, your chance of making a real estate investment significantly below market value is not very good.

Some ads will indicate reasons for selling. Divorce sale, owner transferred, and an imminent foreclosure are reasons why sellers become motivated.

Ads indicating "submit all offers", "asking...", or "OBO (Or Best Offer)," might indicate a motivated seller but could also mean the property is merely overpriced.

Out-of-town homes advertised for rent are usually rented because they cannot be sold. Such owners are an excellent group to contact.

Homes listed for rent or lease option are also an excellent source to investigate. When an owner says, "lease-option" it usually indicates a sale is preferable, buy they are renting because they cannot afford to keep the property vacant.

Properties that have been on the market for a long time and have had several price reductions should also be investigated. When an initial high price is reduced to a more realistic price, it seldom generates the type of interest which an initial low price creates. The owner might just be ready for your offer.

While rent control areas should generally be avoided, rent control *can* provide opportunities. When rent control ordinances are first proposed or passed there are usually a few owners who panic, and who will accept both bargain prices and terms.

Absentee owners of problem properties can be highly motivated to sell. Some investors check the tax assessor's office for absentee owners within an area before calling the owners to determine their interest in selling.

FORECLOSURE SALES

Foreclosures offer very special opportunities for investors. Foreclosure notices are published in legal newspapers and may also be posted at your local courthouse. In some areas, entrepreneurs publish lists of foreclosure property.

Never bid at a foreclosure sale unless you know the condition of the title. When a mortgage is foreclosed it wipes out all junior liens but not liens with a greater priority (tax liens and liens recorded prior to the foreclosing lien). A foreclosure sale might not wipe out IRS liens unless the IRS was properly notified. Therefore, a purchase at a foreclosure sale could give you a property with a number of liens against it. If you failed to pay them, then you could be the one foreclosed.

BUYING RIGHT

To find out what you are actually going to get at foreclosure, you should consider contacting a title company and obtaining a property profile which would show all liens against the property. Some insurers will, for a fee, agree to issue title insurance if you are the buyer, subject to whatever prior liens the property profile reveals. You should also check the redemption rights in your state. In some states, owners have a statutory period to redeem after foreclosure.

If the former owner goes bankrupt within one year of foreclosure, the bankruptcy court could set the sale aside if they determine the sale was for less than fair value.

The foreclosing lienholder might not want the property back. Therefore, you should not open the bidding at the lien amount. Bidders in such situations often buy the property for only 70 to 80 percent of the foreclosing lien.

BEFORE-FORECLOSURE PURCHASES

Often, purchases can be made prior to foreclosure from motivated owners. Sometimes owners will give up their interests just to avoid foreclosure. In other cases an owner will accept a relatively small sum of money, free rent, or promissory notes for their interest. If you are buying prior to foreclosure you should have the title searched.

While a foreclosure wipes out junior liens, a purchase would leave you with all of the liens on the property intact.

Too good a deal could subject you to penalties. In several states it is a violation of the law to take unconscionable advantage of owners in default.

AFTER FORECLOSURE

Some of the best investment opportunities arise *after* property is foreclosed. Lenders will often not only give excellent loan terms to get rid of foreclosed property, but in many cases will even loan the purchaser additional money to rehabilitate the property.

Private lenders who foreclosed on the mortgages they carried back when they sold the property are usually highly motivated. They don't want the property and often cannot afford to keep it.

You should consider contacting the foreclosing lien holder about buying in the event there are no other bidders at the foreclosure sale. The lien holder will generally be receptive to an agreement contingent upon obtaining the property at the sale. An advantage of buying after foreclosure is that you will be able to determine the status of the title prior to closing.

BUYING RIGHT

TAX SALES

Because taxes are priority liens, a purchaser at a tax sale generally gets good title. However, many states allow the homeowner to redeem after the sale. Before you bid at a tax sale you should understand the rights in your state, if any, of the former owner.

Tax sales are usually by assessor's number rather than by street address. You might have to research the locations from the assessor's maps to find out what is being sold. Never bid sight unseen.

SHERIFF'S SALES

These sales are usually held because of judgments against a property. Many states allow a redemption period after the sale so that an owner can redeem by paying you what you paid, plus a statutory interest.

Sheriff's sales only transfer the interests of the debtor. A buyer at a sheriff's sale would get clear title only if the owner had clear title. Check title status prior to bidding at a sheriff's sale.

ESTATE PROPERTY

When there is no surviving spouse, exceptional opportunities can be found in estate properties.

Heirs are often eager for a quick sale. This is especially true when the heirs live outside the property area. County probate records will indicate estates being probated. This information is also available in legal newspapers.

Some buyers include all furniture and personal property in their offers. Heirs often feel relieved about not having to ship or sell the property. Personal property can be a valuable plus when included with the real estate.

UNFINISHED BUILDINGS

Properties where owners have run out of money before completion can offer exceptional opportunities *and* dangers. Prior to any purchase you should consult an attorney and/or obtain title insurance against possible mechanic's liens. You will also want to ascertain the cost of completion by obtaining firm bids for the work.

WHITE ELEPHANTS

A high vacancy factor or other unsolvable problems turn properties into white elephants. Owners will be receptive to any chance to unload this type of property. However, someone else's problems can be *yours,* as well, unless you can solve them.

BUYING RIGHT

Many of the most successful real estate investors are problem solvers. By changing use or by instituting better management they have turned white elephants into sought-after investment property.

Look for properties with large structures that have been vacant for a long period of time. Analyze the problems and consider possible solutions. If you have faith in your ability to solve the problem, then that white elephant could be your investment opportunity.

You should also consider an *option* to purchase rather than a purchase. This will tie up the property for an option fee while you attempt to solve the problems. If you decide not to go through with the purchase, your only loss is the option fee.

You don't have to buy the white elephant to make a profit; a master lease is an alternative to purchase. When there is a high vacancy rate, owners will often look favorably upon an offer to lease all of the vacant space under a long-term lease, even at bargain rent. Using a master lease, you are betting that you will be able to find tenants to sublease.

Your risk can be materially reduced by obtaining an option to lease rather than obligating yourself to the lease itself. If you are unable to sublease, your only loss would be the amount you paid for the option.

BELOW-MARKET RENTS

Owners often set rents from their *impression* of the market, not from market reality. In addition, some owners are lax about reevaluating rent levels. You will therefore find a great variance between rentals being paid by different tenants for similar properties.

Because income-property prices normally relate directly to rents and net income, property having below-market rents would appear to have a lower value. But if rents can be immediately increased, or if leases will be expiring in the near future, it would be possible to dramatically increase the value of property having below-market rents by simply raising the rents.

When you hear of a property having low rents, contact the owner about selling. A reasonable offer based on present rents could well be a fantastic bargain.

FIXER-UPPERS

The fact that property has been allowed to deteriorate generally means there are problems. Fixer-upper properties offer exceptional opportunities for persons willing to spend the time and money to purchase and repair them.

BUYING RIGHT

Buyers for fixer-uppers are limited to those with imagination and a willingness to work. Most prospective buyers can't visualize a property repaired, repainted, with new carpeting and/or tile. They see only a dirty, neglected property. The fact that buyers are limited for this type of property allows purchasers favorable prices and terms.

When bidding on fixer-upper property keep in mind that most people tend to underestimate repair costs by 50 to 100 percent. There are often latent defects not discovered until repair work is underway.

A great many people make their living by buying, fixing, and selling these properties. They generally look for properties which will allow them a minimum of 300 percent profit on the cost of repairs (including the fair value of their labor), plus the costs of holding and resale.

CONSTRUCTION

When land costs and construction costs are significantly less than the sales price of new buildings, value can be created by building. Before you decide to build you should see an attorney about the construction contract. You will want to be protected by a fixed price, definite specifications, and a set completion period. You also want to be assured that you will be protected against mechanic's liens.

WHAT TO OFFER

Try not to fall in love with a property. Your emotions could lead you to pay more than you should because you fear losing the property. Also, showing strong emotion will indicate to an owner or agent that a counteroffer rather than an acceptance is called for. Your emotions can rob you of your bargaining power.

Don't base offers on asking prices. An asking price may bear no relationship to value. It generally indicates what an owner would love to get for the property. Similarly, list prices of similar properties indicate what others are asking. You should be interested in *selling* prices. Selling prices of similar properties are a valid indication of market value.

If the property you are interested in has any deferred maintenance, the cost of the work should be deducted before arriving at an estimation of market value.

You want to buy as much under market as possible. The seller's motivation will be your guide. The greater the motivation to sell, the lower your offer should be. The worst that can happen is a rejection. Even then the owner is likely to make a counteroffer somewhere between your offer and the asking price.

What an owner paid will affect what an owner will accept. Owners are more likely to take a significant price reduction—while still making a profit—than they would if the sale were to result in a loss. It is possible to get a fairly accurate estimate of what the seller paid by checking the seller's deed in the county records.

You should keep in mind that price can be a function of terms. A higher price and more desirable terms can be the equivalent of a lower price and market terms.

Developers in subdivisions do not like to cut prices on one unit, even when they are desperate for a sale. A lower price to one can mean dissatisfaction of other buyers. In lieu of a price cut, developers will often agree to include appliances or to upgrade the unit at a below-market cost.

SEE WHAT YOU
ARE BUYING

With multi-unit properties, unless they are newer units, you will want to see *every* unit, not just those that are vacant or offered to be shown. What you could be shown otherwise are just upgraded units not typical of the property.

PRESSURE SELLING

You should generally walk away when faced with an owner or broker who indicates great urgency to sell. While the now-or-never proposition could be a bargain, it could also be a trap. Never make any purchase decision before you have assured yourself of its economic viability. If a broker or seller does not want to give you the time to obtain expert opinions, you will likely be far better off in turning down the property.

PROTECT YOURSELF

Make sure a property is not in violation of codes. Check the local planning department to ascertain zoning. The building department and fire marshal can tell you about any code violations.

If there have been obvious add-ons, you will want to be certain that building permits were obtained for the work.

You might want to include a statement in your offer that reads, "This offer is contingent upon the property complying with all health, safety, building, and fire codes, and ordinances as to its present use." You could then investigate these before closing.

You might also consider adding "Seller warrants that all mechanical, electrical, and plumbing systems, as well as appliances and fixtures, will be in good and proper working order at time of closing. Purchaser and/or agent shall inspect same and certify compliance or noncompliance by (date). If deficiencies are noted the seller shall have 7 days to correct, or the purchaser shall have the right to cancel this contract without penalty or costs."

In termite areas you might want a termite inspection by a licensed exterminator, and a statement that the property is free of infestation and has no structural damage.

SELLER'S FIGURES

Sellers will often supply figures on income performance which bear little relationship to reality.

Scheduled gross is the gross if all units were rented at the scheduled rents, with no rent concessions or vacancies.

Broker's net income is not truly a net income because it does not include any management charges or factors for vacancies and collection losses.

Average utility costs provided by the seller might be averaged over 10 years, providing a completely unrealistic estimate of what today's costs would be.

Insurance costs don't mean much unless you know the owner's coverage. It may be inadequate; give special attention to the owner's liability coverage.

The owner should write on a copy of his operating statement that the statement is complete and accurate as to all income received and expenses incurred for the period stated. If the owner refuses to sign such an addition, you should place no reliance whatsoever on the operating statement.

It is always a good idea to check with tenants about rents actually paid, as well as any rental concessions which were given. Ascertain also if the tenants are on leases; if so, ask when they expire. When rental concessions are given, the likelihood of tenants leaving upon lease expiration increases. You should also check with the tenants about deposits and rent paid in advance. You might consider having your attorney prepare *estoppel certificates* for the tenants to sign. These show the amount of deposits, prepaid rents, and any other claims they may have. By signing, they are precluded from later raising any additional claim against you.

YOUR OFFER

Familiarize yourself with an offer-to-purchase form. A local Realtor can supply you with a form approved by your State Board of Realtors. It will include any requirements mandated by your state laws. By using the same form for all your offers you are unlikely to be surprised by the agreement you have signed.

While considering an offer, a half hour spent with a real estate attorney will be money well invested. You want to be certain you fully understand all terms and conditions.

You might want escape provisions which would allow you to get out of the purchase under certain circumstances. As an example, you might want the offer contingent upon obtaining a specified loan with specified terms. Keep in mind that the more conditions you apply to your offer, the less the likelihood of acceptance.

You want to make certain there are no agreements left to oral understanding. If it is agreed to, get it in writing.

Keep in mind that a clause printed in an offer form is not cast in stone. You can cross it out.

TIME FOR ACCEPTANCE

Don't give an owner very long for acceptance. One or two days are ample if the owner is available in the same city. If you give too much time, an owner will ask friends and relatives for advice.

The easiest advice to give is, "Oh, you can get more than that!" It might not be true but it will lessen the chance of your offer's acceptance.

Owners will often try to create a sense of urgency by indicating someone else is interested, but you can reverse this tactic to your advantage. Tell the owner or agent the reason you will give only a short period for acceptance is that you are also considering another property and don't want to lose it. This puts the owner in the position of not wanting to lose you as the buyer. Your statement will have been absolutely true because in analyzing and comparing property you will have developed second choices.

EARNEST MONEY

The deposit given with an offer is called *earnest money*. An extremely low offer looks much better with a large earnest-money deposit. Some professional dealers in real property will staple several thousand-dollar bills to their offer. The effect of this on the owner can be enormous.

Never give cash or checks directly to an owner if a broker is not involved in the transaction; there is the possibility the owner will spend the money and be unable to deliver marketable title. If checks are given, they should be made out to an *escrow account,* which is a neutral depository used in some states for real estate closings. Checks

BUYING RIGHT

can also be made out to the trust account of the attorney who is to handle the closing.

PERSONAL PROPERTY

If you want specific personal property included, state this in your offer. Besides avoiding later misunderstandings, you are likely to get what you asked for. Even if an owner refuses to include what you asked for, you can use your request as a concession for negotiation purposes.

DON'T FORGET

Remember that the act of purchasing property costs more than just the selling price. The most significant costs (assuming no capital improvements are necessary after the purchase) are typically the points, commission or loan fee, and incidental loan costs (including appraisal and credit checks) necessitated by institutional financing. These ancillary costs are important in determining your basis for depreciation, and whether or not you will achieve a profit at a certain selling price.

Remember also that laws requiring zoning, foreclosure, bankruptcy, insurance, and other factors that play a part in the purchase of property can vary in different municipalities and states. Many of these factors are covered by federal laws, as well. Be sure to thoroughly investigate laws that will have impact upon your property purchase. Because many of these laws are complex, we recommend that you consult a real estate attorney and/or other qualified experts before committing yourself to a purchase of property.

THE BEST FINANCING TECHNIQUES

An investor can spend a great deal of time locating desirable, advantageously priced investment property, only to be unable to structure financing acceptable to himself or to the seller. Financing is an integral part of any real estate purchase, and can be tailored in many ways to meet your specific needs.

MORTGAGES

Mortgages are the most common security devices used in real estate transactions. The *mortgagor* is the borrower. He or she gives a *lien* or a title to the *mortgagee,* who is the lender. Should the mortgagor default, the mortgagee can foreclose. Foreclosure often allows the purchaser a lengthy period of redemption.

Adjustable-rate mortgages

You should not consider adjustable-rate mortgages unless there is an interest advantage of about 2 percent below fixed-rate mortgages. Do not consider the teaser rates, offered for a few years only, when making your loan decision. Any adjustable-rate mortgage should have a maximum annual increase and a ceiling rate.

BEST FINANCING TECHNIQUES

Adjustable-rate mortgages should not be obtained when the property carries fixed long-term leases; rate increases could result in a serious negative cash flow.

Fifteen-year mortgages

If you intend to hold property for income and appreciation, you should seriously consider a 15-year mortgage. The savings in loan costs can be spectacular.

The monthly payments on a 30-year, 11 percent $100,000 loan would be $952.34. A monthly payment of $1,136.65 would be required to pay off a 15-year loan of the same amount. In other words, a payment of less than 20 percent more each month can pay off the loan in half the time, and reduce interest payments by more than $138,000.

A further advantage of 15-year financing is that lenders will often lower interest by one-fourth to one-half of a percentage point because their risks are reduced.

Blanket mortgages

When you own a number of properties and a lender does not want to give you as large a loan as you desire for a purchase, suggest a blanket mortgage. This type of mortgage would include other properties that you own, giving the lender greater security.

BEST FINANCING TECHNIQUES

Whenever a blanket mortgage is given, be certain that releases clauses are included. These will allow properties to be released from the mortgage upon payment of agreed amounts. Without a release clause, the entire mortgage would have to be paid before you could legally sell a single parcel.

TRUST DEEDS

Trust deeds, sometimes called deeds of trust, are used in some states to finance real estate. The purchaser, who is called the *trustor,* gives a note evidencing the debt to a lender, who is called a *beneficiary,* as security for the note. The trustor gives the title (the trust deed) for holding to a third party. This third party is the trustee. In the event the trustor is in default, the *trustee,* after proper notice, has the right to sell the property. The trustor generally has no rights after this sale. Because of the relatively easy foreclosure, sellers carrying financing under trust deeds are often willing to accept a lower down payment than a seller under a mortgage.

LAND CONTRACTS

Land contracts, or real property purchase contracts, are used in most states. Under these agreements the seller retains title to the property; the buyer obtains only possession. A deed is given when the contract is paid off. State law generally provides for relatively quick foreclosure of the purchaser's interests should there be a default in payments. Because of the easy foreclosure, owners are often willing to sell under land contract with lower down payments than they would require with a mortgage. As a purchaser, you would want to make certain that the seller can deliver marketable title. Land contracts make title insurance available to purchasers.

ADVANCE FEES

Never give anyone an advance fee for promises of spectacular financing. The likelihood of getting any such financing is very slim and you will be out a fee. Be aware, however, that virtually all institutional lenders (banks, savings and loans, etc.) require an application fee that may or may not be refundable in whole.

LOAN ASSUMABILITY

If a loan says nothing about assumability it can be assumed. FHA and VA loans are assumable by any purchaser. However, loans which state they are not assumable or are due in full upon sale may not be assumed.

Some seminar presenters suggest ways to get around due-on-sale clauses, such as unrecorded land contracts and lease options. One of the more

BEST FINANCING TECHNIQUES

innovative suggestions is a friendly foreclosure where the loan amount is really the seller's equity and the lender, by foreclosing, takes title. These methods are likely invitations to a lawsuit. Rather than use subterfuge, consider contacting the lender and offering an interest increase to allow assumption. Lenders will often agree to a rate less than the market rate they are asking for new loans.

SOURCES OF CASH

Many owners of life insurance policies don't realize how inexpensive it is to borrow on their policies. The rates are normally printed on the policies. Older insurance policies have borrowing rates as low as 5 percent.

Other sources of cash include borrowing on stocks and bonds, certificates of deposit, and even on some pension plans. You can also obtain second mortgages or refinance other real estate. Many credit cards authorize cash advances of several thousand dollars. Keep in mind that credit card loans are expensive, and should be used only for short periods.

If you can't borrow cash perhaps you can borrow someone's credit. Perhaps a relative will agree to

BEST FINANCING TECHNIQUES

lend their name to a loan as an accomodation party. Lenders will make loans to persons who ordinarily would not qualify if the application includes an accomodation party with good credit.

Remember that tenant security and rental deposits are turned over to the purchaser at closing. The net effect of this is that the cash required by the purchaser is reduced.

Payment moratorium

If you will be in need of cash after a purchase for repair or other purposes, you should consider an offer where interest and payments on the owner-financing are not to start until several months after closing. This might give you the cash you need.

Owner borrowing

When you have little or no cash and an owner needs a subtantial amount in order to complete a sale, a simple solution is to have the owner either refinance the property with a new assumable loan, or to obtain an assumable second mortgage. The owner keeps the cash that is generated and you assume the loan(s). The balance of the purchase price could be given by you with a new second or third mortgage allowing a no down payment sale.

BEST FINANCING TECHNIQUES

MANUFACTURING PAPER

Sellers often want down payments for security reasons, feeling that a buyer without a down payment is likely to default. If you own other property in which you have an equity, you can meet the seller's needs without cash. Your down payment can be in the form of a second mortgage on the other property you own. The seller has the protection of *two* properties, making default unlikely. You have purchased a property without cash.

PAPER FOR PROPERTY

Sellers will often indicate that they will accept less than a market rate of interest on their owner financing.

If an owner will finance the sale at a below-market rate, then the owner might well accept instead well-secured mortgages on other properties bearing a similar interest in exchange for his or her equity. The trade makes sense because the owner will be getting good mortgages having similar security.

Your advantage is that owner-financed, below-market mortgages can be purchased at less than face value. Twenty to forty percent discounts are not unusual.

BEST FINANCING TECHNIQUES

A new loan of 75 to 80 percent of the purchase price will probably be enough to refinance the property and pay for the mortgages that are exchanged for the seller equity. Not only does this technique allow a low or no down payment, it also allows a significant further reduction in the price negotiated for the property.

Seller discount

While a seller might not grant price reductions at time of purchase, sellers who carry paper will often give a reduction later. Contact the seller after he or she has been receiving your monthly checks for a period of time and indicate that you can arrange to pay off the loan if the seller will grant an agreed-upon discount. The thought of having all the cash at once will often motivate the seller, and work in your favor.

BROKER'S COMMISSION

Sellers often need cash to pay a broker's commission. A low or no down payment offer whereby you will pay the commission will often be received with interest by a seller.

Prior to the offer you will want an agreement with the broker whereby the broker will accept your note for the commission. Many brokers will be receptive to taking paper in lieu of cash for their

BEST FINANCING TECHNIQUES

commission if it means the difference between a paper commission or no commission.

ESCALATING INTEREST OFFER

An owner who indicates that he or she wants cash can sometimes be enticed to carry paper with an escalating interest. As an example, the interest might be 9 percent for the first two years, 10 percent for the next two years, and 15 percent thereafter. The 15 percent figure is the hook that grabs the seller's interest. In actuality, you will have owner financing for four years, after which time you will want to refinance.

LEASE OPTION

Owners who won't sell with a low down payment will often agree to a lease option. You would want as long an option as possible. Even if the option is at market price, inflation could make it a bargain purchase by the time the option is exercised. By that time, a loan for the full purchase price would be possible.

Leases can often be structured so that all or part of the future rent applies to the purchase. In these cases the purchaser would be able to show an actual cash down payment to enable him or her to obtain financing for the balance of the purchase price.

BEST FINANCING TECHNIQUES

A unique advantage of a lease option is that the tenant has full control over the property. If an option is obtained at an attractive price, the tenant can put the property on the market for sale because good title can be delivered by exercise of the option. The tenant not only has occupancy for the rent but the possibility of profit as well. Every renter should try to negotiate a purchase option.

SWEAT EQUITY

When property is in need of repair, sellers can frequently be encouraged to sell with no down payment if the purchaser makes specified improvements prior to closing. (The buyer would want to make certain that the seller can—*and will*—deliver good title). This approach is often receptively received by lenders who have foreclosed on a property. They are saved the problem of putting still more money into that property.

ZERO-COUPON BONDS

Zero-coupon bonds are corporate debentures which may be purchased at deep discounts from the face amount. They pay no interest but do pay face value when due. The sale price of these bonds would be based upon current interest rates, the due date of the bond, and its rating. Bonds are rated according to risk.

BEST FINANCING TECHNIQUES

A number of investors have discovered that zero-coupon bonds are a convenient trading medium to use to purchase real estate. They are most likely to be used when purchasing land. As an example, assume a developer would consider paying $100,000 cash for a commercial lot. Instead, the developer offers a $250,000 zero-coupon bond due in 15 years in exchange for the lot. Chances are that such a bond could be purchased for less than $70,000. If the seller accepts, the developer would have the equivalent of a savings of more than $30,000 from what he or she would have been willing to pay. The seller of the lot would have exchanged a negative cash flow investment (because of taxes) for the promise of a significantly higher payoff 15 years down the road.

By obtaining current bond quotes, you do not have to buy the bonds needed to back your offer until the offer has been accepted.

It is unlikely that owners of income property or homeowners would accept zero-coupon bonds for their property. Land owners are more inclined to accept these offers because they are more likely to own the property free and clear, and are accustomed to a long hold period for appreciation. They are likely to view zero-coupon bonds as a way to lock in a future sale at an agreed price, which provides them with a significant profit as well as an opportunity to pass tax responsibility on to the buyer.

BUY BUILDING ONLY

A commercial property owner who wants a large down payment or even all cash will be intrigued by an offer to buy the building only and lease the land. Owners like the idea that they and/or their heirs will receive land rent, as well as the return of the building when the lease expires.

The benefits to you—other than a purchase with a low down payment—could be land rent lower than the additional debt service if you had purchased the land. Your entire investment would be for improvements, and could be depreciated. Rent for the land would be a fully deductible business expense.

YOUR BEST INVESTMENT

The best real estate investment for you might not be the best investment for your neighbor. Your individual financial status, age, plans, and needs all affect what is best for you.

The following profiles are provided to help you plan the real estate investment program best suited to you.

Profile 1:   The Young Couple

Name	Age	Profession	Earnings
Ben	26	School Teacher	$27,000
Alice	23	Dental Technician	$16,000
			$43,000

Principal assets:

Savings — $3,800
Two late-model cars, neither paid for.
Furniture is paid for.

Specifics: Though Ben and Alice have no children, they would like to start a family within five years. They currently rent at $500 per month, and have been married two years. Their expenses always seem to closely match their income. Ben's salary will increase during the next 6 years to $35,000, plus cost of living raises. There is a mandatory teacher's retirement fund to which he must contribute.

Recommendations: Ben and Alice need a forced savings plan. Purchase of a home with a low down payment would force savings as well as reduce tax liability. In addition, their future housing costs would be locked in.

Both Ben and Alice should start an IRA, preferably in hybrid REITs offering income and appreciation.

Profile 2: The Single Mother

Name	Age	Profession	Income	
Margie	34	Legal Secretary	$18,000 + 5,000 $23,000	child support

Principal assets:

Four-year-old car (paid for). Margie has just received $5,000 as an auto accident settlement.

Specifics: Margie has daughters ages 7 and 12, and currently rents an apartment for $600 per month. She has not been able to save, and has no retirement plan other than Social Security. Margie has no significant debts.

YOUR BEST INVESTMENT

Recommendations: The $5,000 of yearly child support should be invested in either a triplex or fourplex for her family occupancy so that her net housing cost is reduced. Besides offering appreciation in value, the dwelling will increase the quality of her life, and will be paid for by the time she retires. The income will supplement her Social Security. Increased rents in the future will further increase the quality of her life.

Profile 3: The Attorneys

Name	Age	Profession	Earnings
Bill	43	Attorney	$ 78,000
Barbara	43	Attorney	$ 92,000
			$170,000

Principal assets: $120,000 equity in home, $30,000 equity in vacation home, $22,000 in checking and money market accounts, $45,000 in a mutual fund, and $18,000 in an IRA account at a savings and loan.

Specifics: The twins (Bill and Barbara's only children) will be leaving home to start college at State University next year. Both children hope to follow their parents into the legal profession. Previously, the attorneys invested in a limited partnership which purchased a race horse. Unfortunately, the horse died. They also had invested in a cattle feeding partnership which was to have been a fantastic tax shelter. Instead, it resulted in an IRS audit and penalties.

Recommendations: The children will likely be at State University for four years; if they go to law school at State, Bill and Barbara will have to pay tuition an additional three years. With this expense facing them, Bill and Barbara should consider buying a condo as close to the university as possible and rent it to their children, who can take in one or two additional students. An even better alternative might be to purchase an apartment building and have their children manage it, taking an apartment and salary as management fees. Both alternatives would serve to shelter income from taxation, appreciate as investments, and provide for the children's expense.

The attorneys should also consider limited partnership investments with medium and low leverage. Ideally, these investments should offer appreciation, income, and reasonable tax benefits. Bill and Barbara should check out local private offerings as well as public partnerships.

For liquidity, they should balance the limited partnership investments with equity REITs that are approximately 50 percent leveraged for safety, income, and tax benefits.

Their IRA account should be rolled over to a mortgage REIT, which will provide safety as well as increased income.

YOUR BEST INVESTMENT

Profile 4: The Student

Name	Age	Profession	Earnings
Tim	20	Student	$6,100

Principal assets: $2,600 in the bank and a five-year-old van.

Specifics: Tim works in construction during the summer, and for a janitorial company on weekends during the school year. He is paying all of his college expenses and expects to remain in school four to five more years in order to earn an MBA degree.

Recommendations: Tim should look for a fixer-upper house close to campus and use techniques shown in Chapters VII and VIII to purchase the property with no down payment. Sweat equity coupled with appreciation should give Tim a comfortable nest egg by the time he graduates. Tim should enjoy a positive cash flow by renting out rooms to other students.

Profile 5: The Salespersons

Name	Age	Profession	Earnings
John	43	Salesman	$19,000
Emma	44	Sales manager	$42,000
			$61,000

YOUR BEST INVESTMENT

Principal assets: $27,000 in an IRA at a savings and loan, $5,000 in cash deposits, and $16,000 in municipal bonds.

Specifics: The couple has an 8-year-old son. They are renting an apartment for $750 per month.

Recommendations: John and Emma should buy a house or condominium. By selling their municipal bonds for this purpose, they will be ahead tax-wise, and will have gained a capital investment which protects against inflation.

Their IRA should be rolled over into mortgage and equity REITs or into a hybrid REIT having medium leverage. This would offer income, safety, and appreciation.

Profile 6: The Almost-Retirees

Name	Age	Profession	Earnings
Jeff	61	City Employee	$34,000
Peggy	60	Part-time Secretary	6,000
			$40,000

Principal assets: $12,000 in a savings and loan; a city pension which will pay $8,800 per year at age 65 (in addition to Social Security), and a one-year-old automobile.

Specifics: Jeff and Peggy enjoy good health. They have one child, who has recently graduated college and is now married. The couple has always lived in apartments; their current rent is $450 per month. Jeff and Peggy plan to move to Florida when they retire.

Recommendations: Jeff and Peggy can lock in their retirement dream by buying a modest condominium in Florida. A down payment of $8,000 would be sufficient. Income could be created by renting the unit until they retire. They should buy now because there presently is a depressed market for condominiums in Florida. By the time Jeff and Peggy retire, the market could have firmed up; inflation could conceivably make their retirement dream *just* a dream. An immediate purchase would allow the couple to shelter income in what will undoubtedly be their highest-income years. Because their child has completed college, their expenses should be materially reduced; they should consider putting their money to work in an IRA account invested in mortgage REITs. During their final four years of work, Jeff and Peggy could invest $16,000 ($2,000 each, per year) in the REITs.

Profile 7: The Young Professional

Name	Age	Profession	Earnings
Don	36	Advertising Account Executive	$71,000

YOUR BEST INVESTMENT

Principal assets: $31,000 in savings, certificates of deposit, and money market accounts. $8,000 in mutual funds. Ownership of a $45,000 automobile.

Specifics: Don rents a loft for $750 per month. He is a workaholic, whose lifestyle revolves around work and social activities.

Recommendations: Don needs to reduce his taxes and provide for retirement. Investments should be relatively management-free.

Don's first step should be the purchase of a loft condominium or condominium-type apartment. This would allow tax deductions, and act as a hedge against inflation. Such an investment would also provide appreciation possibilities.

Don should establish an IRA in mortgage REITs for greater income. This would shelter $2,000 of income each year.

Annual investments should be divided between equity REITs offering liquidity, and limited partnerships with moderate leverage for tax benefits.

Profile 8: The Former Farmer

Name	Age	Profession	Earnings
Paul	36	Laborer	$19,500
Judy	31	Part-time Waitress	9,000
			$28,500

YOUR BEST INVESTMENT

Principal assets: $3,000 in the bank, a nine-year-old car, and a seven-year-old pickup truck.

Specifics: Paul and Judy have four children, ages 7, 9, 11, and 12. The couple lost their farm two years ago because its income was not sufficient to pay the debt service. Paul is an all-around handyman who works for the city as a general laborer. They currently pay $450 each month to rent a two-bedroom home. The entire family dreams of returning to farming. The $3,000 in savings represents two years of effort.

Recommendations: Paul and Judy will never realize their dream if they try to save part of their salaries. But an investment in fixer-upper real estate could help them achieve their dream. The couple should buy a fixer-upper home, move in, fix it up, and put it on the market for sale. Then they should repeat the process, going to larger homes and even fixer-upper apartment buildings. Their determined effort to save money shows they are willing to sacrifice. What Paul and Judy need now is direction.

Profile 9: The Doctor and the Carpenter

Name	Age	Profession	Earnings
Keith	36	Carpenter	$ 28,000
Libby	38	Plastic Surgeon	$196,000
			$224,000

YOUR BEST INVESTMENT

Principal assets: $150,000 home equity, $130,000 in common stock, $41,000 in municipal bonds, $8,000 in gold, $73,000 in cash and certificates of deposit. Equity of $90,000 in office condo. Libby has $93,000 in her insurance company pension plan.

Specifics: Keith and Libby have two children, a girl age 3 and a boy age 5. They are a very private family. Keith enjoys the children and doing things with his hands. He does all the repair work on the family cars. Libby enjoys being outdoors. She likes to hike and bike. The couple has been thinking about buying a house in the country so they can get away on weekends and vacations.

Recommendations: Instead of a weekend home, Keith and Libby's needs would be better served by a farm. They should consider a large farm approximately an hour from the city. A large farm would provide a needed tax shelter, opportunity for great appreciation, and best of all, a place they would enjoy.

Instead of a professional manager they could consider hiring a farm family. Keith would have plenty of things to fix and do in a comfortable environment. The family would have privacy and a fine place for their children. Because of proximity to the city, the farm, besides offering maximum appreciation potential, could possibly become their principal residence.

YOUR BEST INVESTMENT

Keith should set up an IRA, preferably in a REIT.

Additional investments in private and public limited partnerships should be considered.

Profile 10: The Traveler and the Artist

Name	Age	Profession	Earnings
Ted	29	Sales Representative	$47,000
Anne	29	Artist	6,800
			$53,800

Principal assets: $19,000 in mutual funds, $6,000 in savings accounts, and a company retirement plan which requires two more years before it is a vested interest (current value: $7,300).

Specifics: Ted and Anne have two boys, ages 6 and 4. The couple currently rents a large older home for $680 per month. Ted travels during the week, covering a two-state area. She loves animals. Ted enjoys gardening, hunting, fishing, riding, and motorcycles.

Recommendations: Anne and Ted should consider not just the purchase of a home but a rural home and acreage, or small farm. It would allow them to enjoy their special interest, provide tax deductions, and offer them opportunity for investment appreciation. They should also each set up an IRA account investing in medium to low-leveraged equity REITs or mortgage REITs.